BUCKET
~ TO ~
GREECE

Volume 6

V.D. BUCKET

Copyright © 2020 V.D. Bucket
All rights reserved.

No part of this publication may be reproduced, distributed, or transmitted in any form or by any means, including photocopying, recording, or other electronic or mechanical methods, without the prior written permission of the publisher, except in the case of brief quotations embodied in critical reviews and certain other noncommercial uses permitted by copyright law.

All names have been changed to spare my wife embarrassment.

Editor: James Scraper
Cover: German Creative
Interior Format: The Book Khaleesi

Other Books in the Bucket to Greece Series

Bucket to Greece Volume 1

Bucket to Greece Volume 2

Bucket to Greece Volume 3

Bucket to Greece Volume 4

Bucket to Greece Volume 5

Bucket to Greece Collection Vols 1-3

Chapter 1

A Place to Escape

"I'm at the end of my tether Victor. I don't know how much more of that thoroughly ghastly woman I can take, she sets my teeth on edge," Barry groaned in complaint, grasping his already unruly hair between tightened fists, the dark circles under his eyes accentuating his stressed out state.

"I can imagine. I wonder if she had a face like a slapped trout before she met Lester or whether she grew into it when she took the name Trout," I pondered aloud. Selecting a bottle of Lidl red from the new ornate wine rack intended to give the impression that the downstairs storage area had more than mere pretensions of being an actual wine cellar, I poured Barry a generous measure.

"I'm just glad we finished converting the swimming pool into an ecological pond before the Trouts arrived. Luckily she finds the pond objectionable, otherwise she'd be lazing around on a sun lounger demanding Cynthia serve her poolside cocktails. I've never met anyone so entitled."

"What is her objection to the pond?" I asked, thinking Cynthia had done a marvellous job overseeing the creation of a natural oasis of calm. A carpet of wild flowers replaced the former tiled patio surround and the pond water was a haven for chirping and croaking creatures; I consider the melodic sounds very soothing.

"She has a keen antipathy to frogs, she complains they are disgusting dirty creatures that stink," Barry said, knocking back the contents of his glass.

"Such ignorance," I said. "Frogs may emit a rather pungent odour, but on-going research reveals they harbour skin secretions which show encouraging signs of having antimicrobial peptides."

"You've lost me Victor."

"The secretions the frogs release could be developed into antibiotics. Considering the alarming spread of antibiotic resistant superbugs you will actually be doing a service to science if you encourage your frogs to breed," I said.

"They seem pretty keen on breeding without any encouragement from me. Still if frogs are handy at shifting germs I could sneak one into Mrs Trout's bed and tell her it's our latest cleaning gadget. I'm sick to death of hearing about her fancy new Roomba," Barry chortled.

"Quite. Marigold has been pestering me for an autonomous robotic vacuum cleaner ever since she had coffee with the ghastly woman. I very much doubt a Roomba would make hygienic inroads into the corners," I said. "I think I've managed to spare my credit card by convincing Marigold that she'll spend an age unclogging cat hairs from the device, Clawsome's hairs are noticeably long."

"I can't help feeling a bit sorry for Lester; he's the personification of a henpecked husband and that perpetual twitch of his doesn't help, it makes him look really shifty. I wonder if he constantly twitched before he met his wife or if she just brings it out in him."

"Marigold was under the delusion that he was winking at her excessively before she twigged he had a twitch…"

"Well it is rather unnerving and takes a bit of getting used to," Barry said.

"Send Lester over here, being henpecked he can perhaps bond with the inhabitants of the henhouse," I quipped. It had been difficult to form an impression of Lester beyond noting he was obviously browbeaten, a thin weasel-like man overshadowed by his overbearing wife. "How is Cynthia coping?"

Although my interactions with the Trouts had thus far been limited I hadn't failed to notice how Cynthia's mother was wearing her down, constantly undermining her daughter by criticising everything from Cynthia's decision to settle down in a remote mountain village in Greece, to her parenting skills. The Trout woman made no attempt to disguise the rather askance looks she fired in Barry's direction as she weighed him up, the contemptuous sneer on her lips indicating she found him distinctly lacking.

BUCKET TO GREECE (VOL. 6)

"Cyn is relieved to be going back to work tomorrow, even though it is only part-time. Although she hates the thought of leaving the baby she can't wait to escape her mother. We're both hoping that once Anne is faced with the reality of actually changing a nappy tomorrow she'll start thinking about returning to England. Perish the thought she has to get her hands dirty or lift a finger to help. We must persuade Marigold that it is for the greater good if she doesn't rush over to help out with the baby until I've got rid of the in-laws," Barry sighed.

"You know how Marigold dotes on Anastasia," I said.

"The greater good Victor," Barry reiterated.

I could sympathise with Barry's point. His mother-in-law was a disruptive force seemingly hell-bent on spreading disharmony in his household. Barry was already beginning to hint how comfortable the sofa-bed in my office looked. I worried that if he had to endure Mrs Trout's presence for much longer he and Cynthia might not make it to their one year wedding anniversary next month.

Recalling their wedding day I smiled; Cynthia's bout of pre-wedding nerves had resulted in the birth of an adorable baby girl just three months ago. Agreeing on a name for the new born had thrown up some challenges. Whilst both Barry and Cynthia were eager to embrace Greek traditions, Cynthia flatly refused to follow the custom of naming the baby after Barry's deceased mother Gladys, likewise rejecting my suggestion that they opt for Beryl after Barry's aunt. Although I suspected Cynthia simply didn't fancy lumbering the baby with the old fashioned name Gladys, I did support her point that it might prove a bit of a tongue twister for the Greeks.

Whilst the naming quandary was in full swing I ran into an ex-pat living on the coast. He told me that he'd had the most terrible time sorting out his residency permit since the Greek police couldn't get their tongues around Hugh, the locals repeatedly confusing his name with huge. Because of his bulk he ended up with the nickname *Terastios*, the literal Greek translation of huge: it didn't sit well with him as he was very sensitive to any references pertaining to his weight. Barry and Cynthia finally agreed on Anastasia, a Grekified version of Anne, Cynthia's mother's name. It certainly has an elegant enough ring to appeal to the social climber's grandiloquent tendencies.

BUCKET TO GREECE (VOL. 6)

Mrs Trout's acute fear of flying had prevented Barry's in-laws from rushing over for the birth of their new granddaughter, or of being of any practicable use to Cynthia immediately following the birth. Instead they had arrived in Meli ten days ago, having made their way across Europe at a snail's pace by train and bus, taking the most circuitous route possible through Paris, Berlin, Budapest, and northern Greece, with plenty of leisurely stopovers at nice hotels so they didn't exhaust themselves.

Lester seemed bearable in small doses, if one discounted his vocal gripe that Barry's house lacked a satellite dish; he was apparently keen to follow the current European Football Championship. The whole continent appeared to be in the grip of football fever. Whilst having no interest whatsoever in a bunch of overpaid sportsmen kicking a ball I do feel it is my patriotic duty to support the Greek underdogs whenever the topic arises in the local taverna.

"I'm taking a coachload of tourists to Vathia tomorrow so I'll give Cynthia a lift up to the office. It may give her the chance to catch up on her sleep in the car," I offered.

"She'll appreciate that Victor; we're both completely sleep deprived at the minute and having to give up our bedroom to the Trouts hasn't helped," Barry moaned, a distinctly murderous look in his eyes. Taking a deep breath he changed the subject. "Vangelis tells me he's finished knocking up that grape arbor in your garden so we can drag this old tub of Harold's out of storage later."

"Best wait until dark, I don't want Guzim spotting it and getting any ideas," I cautioned, casting a glance at the bath that Barry had salvaged from his bathroom. I was itching to get it into place and indulge in my improvised outdoor spa.

"Fair point. Marigold will have kittens if she catches the Albanian shed dweller enjoying an al-fresco bubble bath in your garden," Barry said, pulling the dust sheet off the large cast iron tub. "Speaking of kittens, what's this chap doing hiding out in here? I thought you'd given him away to a good home."

"Pickles can hardly be considered a kitten anymore, but he does appear to have an inbuilt homing device. I'm rather resigned to being stuck with him." In truth I had grown quite fond of Pickles, though he does exhibit a tendency to follow me around like a devoted lap-dog. Marigold says I only have myself to blame since I spoil it by feeding it with sardines instead of proper tinned cat food. Pickles is very partial to sardines, though it did inexplicably turn its nose up at the job-lot with added chillies that I bought on special offer in Lidl.

"If we put the bath in place under cover of darkness Guzim might not notice it unless he spots the hosepipe trailing down from the bathroom window," Barry agreed.

My brother-in-law and Vangelis had tackled most of the renovation work on Barry's new home, spurred on to complete the job before the baby arrived. As the lucky recipient of the oversized bath tub that had been replaced by a shower I was looking forward to experimenting with outdoor bubble baths; it had been thoroughly scoured with Vim to eradicate all trace of Harold and Joan wallowing in its depths. Marigold delights in ridiculing my desire, even going as far as looking up and quoting statistics pertaining to the number of bacteria ridden dead skin cells I will be submerged in after sloughing them off.

My wife's ridicule has failed to dampen my enthusiasm; ever since moving to Greece I have missed a good long soak. I finally got my own way over the garden tub by resorting to a spot of bribery, forking out for the installation of an air conditioning unit in our bedroom. It does tend to get very hot at night at this time of year.

Although it was much cooler in the shuttered gloom of the downstairs storage, it was hardly the most comfortable of hide-outs. I was not unaware of the irony that whilst Barry and I both have perfectly lovely village houses, of late we are reduced to slinking off here, Barry to put some much needed distance between himself and Cynthia's mother, while on this occasion I was avoiding Doreen who was giving a passable impression of taking up residence in our kitchen.

"Fancy another drop of wine Barry?" I offered.

"Better not, it wouldn't do to be drunk in charge of the baby. I want to call in on Vangelis on the way home and broach the subject of whether he and Athena would like to be godparents."

"I'm certain they'd be delighted, but surely there's no rush," I said, knowing that Cynthia wanted to wait until Anastasia was a little older before going ahead with her baptism.

"We'd both prefer to wait. It seems a bit of an ordeal to have a tiny baby submerged in an oil filled font, but Cynthia's mother has been making noises about wanting to attend the christening. The longer we delay it the longer we might end up stuck with the Trouts, it's not as though they've got a plane to catch," Barry said pragmatically.

"But if you rush into it you risk putting Marigold's nose out of joint," I reminded him. "You know how she feels about being godmother."

"I'm not insensitive to her feelings, but we both know she's never going to do the necessary and convert to Greek Orthodox," Barry sighed, rolling his eyes. Although Barry and Cynthia weren't of the orthodox persuasion they could still have the baby baptised in the Greek Church if they rounded up some orthodox godparents.

"I keep telling her she's too old anyway..."

"I'm sure that goes down well," Barry snorted.

"She needs to face facts. Anastasia needs someone younger than us in the role, especially as you're not exactly a spring chicken yourself. Athena and Vangelis are only in their forties..."

"I'll have a word with Marigold; tell her the pair of you can be honorary godparents without the official title."

"It may help your cause if you bring Anastasia

round later; you know how Marigold can't resist her."

"She's already got you both wrapped round her little finger," Barry observed, his voice bursting with paternal pride.

"I'll not deny that." Anastasia's arrival had been a blessing, enriching all our lives. Marigold and I had resigned ourselves to the idea that Benjamin, being out and proud, was unlikely to present us with a grandchild, and now Anastasia was here to fill the gap. "Did I mention that Guzim is increasing his brood?"

"More rabbits for Cynthia's vile cat to torment," Barry said.

"No, he got Luljeta pregnant again on his last trip home to Albania. I think he wants me to be the godfather, either that or a piggy bank; apart from the position of the stress accent the two Greek words are almost identical and half the time Guzim makes no sense at all with his guttural mumbling."

"A home in a shed and five kids to support, I think it's a safe bet that he's got his sights on you as his personal piggy bank," Barry guffawed.

Chapter 2

Psarosoupa with a French Twist

Barry had already made his way home, promising to sneak back under the cover of darkness to help me drag the bathtub into a secluded position behind the new grape arbor. Biding my time I waited for the coast to clear, having no desire to be pounced upon by Doreen. The rattle of the gate alerted me to the departure of Marigold's ex-pat friend. A screech from the street when Doreen yelled up something completely inane to my wife demonstrated the woman's lack of respect for keeping noise pollution down during the prescribed siesta hours. Peering through the latticed shutters I breathed a sigh of relief as I watched her shuffle off.

My spirits soared as I stepped into the garden, taking the time to stop and smell the roses. It was a perfect June day, wispy white clouds drifting playfully across the blue sky, a slight breeze offering welcome relief from the heat that enveloped me as soon as I left the cool environ of the storage room. I made a mental note to check the weather forecast for the next day; it wouldn't do to be caught out without a brolly if a sudden, though unlikely shower, appeared on the Vathia horizon. The austere beauty of the deep Mani never fails to move me and I was quite looking forward to the trip. The excursion tends to attract the type of tourists who appreciate the fascinating history of the area and the ready snippets of knowledge I am able to impart. I find it quite gratifying to cast my eye over the customer satisfaction surveys and read that my charges are most impressed with the wealth of information I share.

The wonderful scent of lemon thyme and sage assailed my senses, the release of their herby fragrances alerting me that Guzim was probably hovering somewhere nearby with his watering can. Since I was in no mood to be assailed by the shabby Albanian shed dweller I hastily broke off a stem of vibrant orange roses to present to Marigold as a romantic gesture.

An unpleasant fishy aroma permeated the kitchen where Marigold was clattering around, gravitating between tending to something on the hob and wiping down surfaces with a rather dubious looking sponge.

"Ah there you are Victor, where on earth have you been hiding? Oh for heaven's sake, don't bring those roses in here, the last thing we need is another mite infestation. I'm beginning to understand why the Greeks favour plastic flowers for interior décor."

The sound of Marigold's chattering voice followed me as I hurriedly lobbed the roses back into the garden. On my return to the kitchen Marigold thrust a loaded fork under my nose, saying, "Taste this Victor, tell me what you think."

The contents of the fork were unspeakably vile, though I had no clue what dish Marigold had botched. Nevertheless I attempted to conceal my wince of disgust, having no wish to hurt Marigold's feelings if she was trying out a new recipe for something special.

"The flavour is a tad overwhelming," I said noncommittally, discreetly removing a fish bone from my mouth.

"Well they do seem to enjoy their food with a bit of a kick."

"They?" I asked in confusion.

"The cats, I'm experimenting with homemade cat paté from the fish that was leftover from last night."

"Seriously, you are expecting me to taste test pet food. That's rather your department than mine," I complained, reflecting that my wife had a nerve banning fry ups due to the lingering smell when she was prepared to stink out the kitchen by cooking fish that I suspected had definitely turned. "I wouldn't risk this stuff on your precious felines unless you are prepared to spend the evening mopping up cat sick."

"I wasn't sure if it was edible or not, that's why I asked for your opinion Victor," Marigold said, adopting a haughty tone.

"You could always slip it into a Tupperware dish and take it over to Barry's place. Cynthia's foul cat isn't known for its discerning palate," I suggested with an evil grin.

"Cynthia has enough on her plate without

cleaning up cat vomit," Marigold snapped. "She must be in a terrible state with the thought of leaving the baby tomorrow; I remember the torment the first time I had to leave Benjamin."

"But you never left him until he started infant school," I reminded her, recalling Benjamin getting ready for his first day in short trousers, his little face so excited. He was too young to be aware of his pudding basin haircut, though when he looked back on the photograph he chided Marigold for sending him out in public sporting such a fashion travesty.

"It was still a wrench. At least Cynthia has us all to rally round, though for the life of me I still can't imagine why she wants to get back to work so soon," Marigold said. Cynthia had been a bit on the fence about returning to work with the baby just three months old, only reaching a firm decision when her mother turned up, proving to be more critical than supportive.

"It's only part-time; she quite enjoys her job and would probably go mad being stuck at home in a village full of pensioners."

"Now Victor, you know the population of Meli is getting younger, that handsome bee fellow isn't a day over thirty," Marigold argued.

"I hardly think that Barry would be tickled

pink if Cynthia sought out his company..."

"Oh what a lot of nonsense you spout, Giannis wouldn't look twice at Cynthia, he's dating a very attractive girl."

"The girl on the back of his motorbike? I have it on good authority that she's a supermodel, she's certainly got the legs for it," I said recalling the leggy young woman I'd spotted riding pillion. She had caused quite a stir amongst the old codgers playing tavli outside the village store when Giannis roared up on his motorcycle, her bikini clad bosom pressed into the back of his leather jacket, her long raven hair flowing freely as she flouted the helmet law. "I shouldn't think Meli gets many supermodels, being a bit lacking in the yacht and Ferrari department."

"Now you haven't forgotten that we're hosting the meeting of the ex-pat dining club tomorrow evening," Marigold said.

I stared at my wife blankly; I could swear this was the first time I'd heard her mention it, though I must admit to a naturally tendency to tune out whenever the subject rears its tedious head. Doreen had hosted the last event, serving up some suspect slop she tried to pass of as Mongolian. Of course as none of us had ever tasted food originating from the grassland steppes of the exotic Asian country Doreen was able to claim her cooking was authentic, though I rather doubt that Atora suet is a vital ingredient in traditional Mongolian dumplings.

I recalled being trapped at the end of the table next to Norman, bored into an almost catatonic stupor as he droned on about his mind-numbing hobby of collecting traffic cones. Unable to tolerate yet another mention of witches' hats I had abruptly excused myself, claiming I needed to dash home to walk Pickles. Mortified by my rudeness Marigold had insisted on buying a dog lead the next day, forcing me to drag a reluctant cat across the village square to avert Doreen's suspicions that I had invented a convenient excuse to escape.

"Who are we hosting this time?" I asked.

"Doreen and Norman of course, and Milton and Edna. I also invited Sherry and Felix..."

"The names don't ring a bell," I said.

"Oh Victor, I sometimes wonder if you ever listen. Sherry and Felix are the couple who bought that old house that Barry and Vangelis are renovating. I ran into Sherry in the village store and she told me she was eager to meet some new people."

"Ah yes, I remember now, Barry seems to think that they're a bit odd. I've spotted the husband out taking early morning walks, looks a bit strange all kitted out in some ridiculous safari outfit."

"Well let's give them the benefit of the doubt. They've been so busy settling in that they haven't had chance to meet people yet, you remember what it's like when one first makes the move over," Marigold said.

"Hectic times indeed," I agreed, recalling our first month in Meli had been a whirlwind of activity sorting out all the legalities.

"I've invited Anne and Lester Trout to join us as well; I did rather take to Anne. It will be fascinating to hear more about their travels across Europe. When I had coffee with Anne she recommended some lovely hotels we could try if we ever decide to explore the continent by train."

Raising my eyebrows I said "You mean she actually has another topic of conversation beyond her precious Roomba?"

"Don't be silly darling; she had plenty to say about their journey over here and was quite persuasive about the advantages of bussing it."

I didn't bother responding, knowing full

well that Marigold would never willingly travel by public transport. Hating the thought of being herded in with the rabble she had flatly refused to join one of my guided coach tours, even though I had managed to wangle her a free ticket.

"Lester seems to be a bit lacking in the personality department, I expect that infernal twitch of his makes him feel self-conscious," Marigold continued.

"Well make sure you seat him next to Norman, the pair of them will probably get on like a pair of damp squibs," I advised.

"I do hope Barry and Cynthia can make it, I'd love to see Anastasia. She's so cute I could just eat her up," Marigold gushed.

My quip that I hoped Marigold wasn't planning to put the baby on the menu was met with a withering look; admittedly it was a tad juvenile. "Speaking of menus, what are you planning to serve up?" I asked.

"I was rather relying on you Victor. You usually take the lead when we host a dinner party these days."

"Don't look at me. I've got a busy day repping tomorrow. The Vathia excursion usually leaves me dead on my feet. It is a long trip and all the probing questions about the history of the area will keep me constantly on my toes, I won't get a moment to relax."

"I was rather counting on you," Marigold wheedled.

"Well I'm afraid in this instance you must count me out. Try keeping it simple, perhaps just throw something in the slow cooker," I advised.

"Thomas comes through with fresh fish in the morning. Can you give me your recipe for fish soup? One pot cooking would indeed keep it simple and I can serve it with crusty bread and salad."

"My recipe is for Greek *psarosoupa*, I thought the whole idea of the dining club is to serve up meals from different countries," I pointed out.

"Well it is, but I doubt that the Trouts will be able to tell the difference between *psarosoupa* and a French bouillabaisse, don't forget this trip to Greece is the first time they've ventured abroad."

"They aren't the only guests," I reminded her.

"Doreen will be clueless, you know how unspeakably awful her cooking is, and Milton and

Edna will just be grateful to have a proper meal instead of scraps," Marigold said.

"If you get some fresh mussels and squid from Thomas you could pass the *psarosoupa* off as the Spanish stew Zarzuela de Mariscos," I suggested.

"In almost two years of living here I have yet to have as much as a sniff of a fresh mussel from Thomas' van, and if you think I'm messing about with a recently deceased squid you must want your head examining," Marigold scoffed.

"*Psarosoupa* posing as bouillabaisse it is then, I'll dig out my recipe for you," I conceded.

Chapter 3

Milton has Mail

Whilst Marigold cooled off in the shower, I took advantage of her absence to give the sponge a good bleaching, despairing of my wife's lackadaisical approach to basic sponge sanitation. No matter how many times I offer advice on best hygiene practices to avoid the rampant multiplication of bacteria on soggy sponges, she simply does not grasp the concept of a good wringing out. The lingering aroma of rancid cat paté had put me off the idea of cooking: my suggestion that we dine in the taverna later was accepted with enthusiasm.

"Anyone home?" a voice called out. Recognising Milton's plummy vowels I responded in the affirmative, resigning myself to delaying my planned perusal of my well-thumbed copy of Patrick Leigh Fermor's 'Mani'. I find the book a great source of fascinating details about Vathia and always give credit to the author when I regale my tourist charges with any of his literary gems. I find that his account of nailing the severed heads of one's enemies to walls always goes down particularly well since people do tend to love a bit of historical gore. The day-trippers who have heard of the esteemed author and resistance fighter are particularly impressed when I mention I almost rubbed shoulders with him last autumn when we were both taking coffee in the same café close to the *Dimarcheio*. After agonising over interrupting him I reluctantly decided against it, having no wish to come across as a celebrity groupie. If only I'd had my copy of 'Mani' on my person I could have broken the ice by asking him to autograph it.

"Would you like to join me on the balcony for a glass of ouzo?" I invited Milton.

"Don't mind if I do old chap, just the ticket, what," Milton agreed. Noticing that my visitor was clutching a pile of envelopes I hoped they had something to do with his impromptu visit. My patience was wearing thin with the rather feeble excuses he made for constantly dropping by when his pretext was invariably to glean more information about my mother, well out of Edna's earshot. Nevertheless I steered the conversation to small talk about the weather until we'd made a dent in our drinks.

"Wouldn't mind a spot of advice old chap," Milton said once we'd exhausted the weather. "My publisher has forwarded some fan mail addressed to Scarlett Bottom and I'm not sure if it's the done thing to reply. I'm worried the postmark may give away my location in Meli if I respond."

"It could be a tad embarrassing if a load of frustrated housewives descend on the village only to discover Scarlett Bottom is in fact an expat pensioner of the male persuasion," I mused tactfully, biting my tongue to avoid blurting out that his fan club was more likely to comprise the dirty mac brigade.

'Delicious Desire', Milton's book of pornographic scribblings, had recently been published

BUCKET TO GREECE (VOL. 6)

by a US-based purveyor of titillating titles he'd discovered on the internet, bringing a modicum of fame to his pseudonym and attracting interest in the mysterious Scarlett Bottom. Unfortunately for Milton his foray into erotica hadn't yet materialised into quite the money spinner he'd hoped, the publisher offering only a miniscule advance and a vague promise of paltry royalties.

Nevertheless it was quite an achievement for Milton to have a published book under his belt and he was already making noises about penning a sequel. I sympathised with the inevitable frustration he must feel in not being able to boast about his smutty success. I could well end up in the same boat if my recently completed book about our moving to Greece exploits enjoys similar success, with all the adulation directed towards the elusive V.D. Bucket, rather than in my direction. Still my reasons are sound for dusting off the old name I had ditched for real life purposes due to its association with my being abandoned in a bucket at the railway station. Its usage would conceal my true identity and prevent Marigold from becoming a laughing stock.

"I can't quite find the words to describe the

feelings I experienced when this first batch of fan mail arrived, brought I bit of a lump to the old throat don't you know," Milton said. His words made me recall that Cynthia had mentioned that the pages of 'Delicious Desire' did tend to overrun with superfluous cheesy clichés and a significant repetition of a limited amount of descriptive adjectives. Fortunately Marigold had refrained from offering her inexpert literary advice during the course of Milton's writing, thus he was spared her recommendation of littering the pages with excessive exclamation marks.

Eager to boast, Milton proffered the bundle of letters he was clutching. "Would you like to take a look at my fan mail?" Sensing my reluctance to take hold of the envelopes he appeared a tad deflated so I grudgingly grabbed them to avoid causing offence. He could hardly be expected to realise that my disinclination to handle the letters was due to my natural reservation about touching something so potentially grubby without first encasing my hands in protective disposable gloves. I dreaded to think what dubious bodily emissions the readers of such smut may have smeared on their correspondence.

As I leafed through Milton's mail I couldn't

help jumping to the conclusion that his 'fans' were actually a bored intern employed by his publisher, most likely told to write some gumf to massage Milton's ego. Whilst I cannot claim to be an expert graphologist it didn't take a genius to realise that the handwriting of Dolores from Cleveland was almost indistinguishable from that of Cath in Chicago, and Philip in Casper, Wyoming.

"Perhaps you should take the advice of your publisher on whether to respond or not," I suggested. Not wishing to burst his bubble that he had a throng of fans, I played along. "Personally I think it could be a tad risky striking up a correspondence with people of unknown character. After all you know nothing about them beyond their liking for porn."

"Erotica old chap, erotica," Milton remonstrated.

"Even so – I need a shower after reading what Philip from Casper would like to do to Brandy…it does sound terribly grubby."

"You've got him all wrong; my fan Philip has simply copied the passage from my book that he most enjoyed…"

"Well as I've told you a hundred times Milton, erotica really isn't my cup of tea. It's all a bit too racy for me and out of my comfort zone. My taste in literature leans more to the era when table legs were covered up to spare a maiden's blushes, rather than anything more suggestive," I said firmly. Cynthia certainly had a point when she said Milton wrote in clichés; it hardly demonstrated great imagination to rustle up a porn character named Brandy.

An uneasy silence descended between us, fortunately relieved by the arrival of Catastrophe who wasted no time getting her paws on a fan letter and turning it into an improvised scratching pad. Marigold's favoured feline has a distinct weakness for shredding anything paper based, whilst Clawsome much prefers to give our coir doormat a good mauling. Watching Catastrophe work her damage on Milton's letter I made a mental note to search out a new doormat next time we are in town since Catastrophe's claws have made a veritable *kleftiko* of the decorative sheep adorning our current one. I suppressed a giggle at my rather clever mental gymnastics, imagining the abstract sheep served up in the popular paper wrapped Greek lamb dish, aromatically flavoured with lemon, herbs and garlic.

"How's your mother keeping, marvellous

woman?" Milton asked, failing miserably in his attempt to sound nonchalant.

"Let me just get some more ice for the ouzo before I fill you in," I hedged, disappearing to thoroughly scrub my hands in the kitchen before making a beeline for the freezer.

Milton had made a point of swerving Barry's wedding to avoid running into Violet Burke whilst in Edna's company. Amazingly he had never mentioned a word to his wife about his six-decade infatuation with the woman he'd briefly run into in the Pelican, more popularly known as the Dirty Bird, during the war. After catching sight of the object of his fawning devotion in my kitchen Milton had duly fessed up to Edna to spare any embarrassment should the pair of them chance to run into my mother during her holiday in Meli, ignorant of the fact that Violet Burke's recollection of their previous encounter was non-existent.

It was just as well that Milton came clean with his wife since the couple did indeed run into my mother in the days following the wedding. Milton's usual sanguine demeanour deserted him, reducing him to a tongue-tied blushing fool the moment he bumped into Violet Burke at the cheese counter in the village store.

V.D. BUCKET

Fortunately as I was with my mother at the time I was able to do my best to smooth things over, making introductions all round. Even after Milton reminded my mother that they had met in the Pelican, Violet Burke still didn't recall ever meeting him, not because her mind isn't as sharp as a tack but because Milton was too much of a sap to have left a lasting impression and she had been rather free with the kisses she'd exchanged in pursuit of coveted nylons.

Thinking it best to avert any awkwardness I suggested we all grab a coffee outside the shop, doubting that Milton's fanciful crush would actually survive an up-close encounter with my mother; he would surely realise that the striking red-head of his memories had morphed into a bulbous and over-bearing harridan. After Milton had confessed to his wife that he had kissed Violet Burke many moons ago, Edna was naturally wary of the perceived competition for her husband's affection. Edna, who usually comes across as a sweet elderly lady, unleashed an inner snobbishness that instantly rubbed Violet Burke up the wrong way.

Whilst Milton did a passable impression of Sami by remaining mute, the two women made small talk, or more accurately sniped at one

BUCKET TO GREECE (VOL. 6)

another. Edna lost no time in making some condescendingly rude remarks when Violet Burke mentioned that she kept herself busy by working in a chip shop. Shocked by Edna abandoning her usual good manners, I bristled on my mother's behalf. How dare the jumped-up wife of a pornographer look down her nose at my mother; whilst admittedly Vi can be a tad vulgar she is the salt-of-the-earth type and she has not had an easy life. Before I could intervene in her defence Violet Burke gave Edna as good as she got, proclaiming, "There's nothing wrong with doing an honest day's work in the chippy, at least I have my pride and don't have to resort to subsisting on charity hand-outs of cakes from the neighbours." Clearly she still harboured a grudge over the disappearance of the lemon drizzle she'd fancied for her elevenses.

With Violet Burke at her most bolshie I had presumed that Milton would come to his senses and realise his infatuation had no grounding in reality. Now, a year later, he still struggled to relinquish his dreams of the girl who had captivated his attention on the dance floor so long ago, even though Violet Burke in the flesh was nothing like the image embedded in his heart. He had tried to explain his feelings, telling me he was so accustomed to carrying a torch that he felt he would lose a part of himself if he extinguished the flame.

Whenever Milton cornered me without Edna in tow he never lost an opportunity to ask me how my mother was getting on. Keeping his questions to the present I surmised he was at last beginning to get a grip on reality, aware that Violet Burke was not in reality the inamorata of his youthful fantasies. In turn I only offered snippets about her current life, choosing to leave Milton ignorant about my only recently discovered relationship with my mother. I had no wish to divulge family secrets that would leave me exposed to tasteless bucket jokes.

Dropping a couple of ice-cubes into Milton's glass I admitted that I was a tad worried about my mother's living arrangements over the chip shop. Before I had chance to expound the reasons for my concern, Milton interrupted. "She shouldn't be slaving away in a chippy at her age; she ought to be taking it easy."

"Well it appears she could be out of a job very soon," I sighed. I agreed with Milton that my mother deserved to be taking things a bit easier, but she prefers to plod on; it gives her something to have a good moan about and I think she secretly revels in her long-standing rivalry with Mrs Billings who pops in every Friday for battered haddock. Even though standing behind the counter frying chips, battering fish and serving up mushy peas plays havoc with her swollen feet, she does enjoy exchanging a bit of banter with the regulars.

"A developer has bought up the terrace where mother lives, he is trying to get planning permission to demolish the row that houses the chip shop and knock up some new builds; you know the type, overpriced identical boxes with no character. The demise of the chippy will be the end of an era for my mother, leaving her out of a job and a home."

"Couldn't imagine anything worse than being cooped up in one of those modern boxes, one hears dreadful tales of snagging lists left unfinished and not enough room to swing a cat," Milton huffed. "But surely the council will be obliged to re-house her, considering her age."

"I expect so, but she likes it where she is. She finds the thought of moving most unsettling; she's rather a creature of habit."

The previous summer I had flown back to England with my mother, hot on the trail of my other absconded parent. Mother insisting I stay

V.D. BUCKET

with her in the flat over the chippy gave me the opportunity to experience her home and her workplace first hand. Whilst there was no denying the area was a tad rough I had been amazed by the chip shop; it was undoubtedly the cleanest and most hygienic take-away establishment I had ever encountered during all my years of conducting stringent public health inspections. Dot, my mother's co-worker, gave full credit to Violet Burke for the immaculate state of the premises, telling me "It would have been more than my life's worth to let standards slip while she was away. She can't half let rip if anyone slacks on the elbow grease."

The flat above the chippy was decidedly dated in décor and style, but as neat as a pin. I was touched to discover a framed photograph of myself took pride of place on the well-polished mantelpiece, alongside one of Benjamin. Whilst I could appreciate my mother had carved out a pleasant home for herself I struggled to cope with the all-pervasive smell of fried chips lingering in every corner, permeating everything from the lumpy chintz covered sofa that had seen better days, to the candlewick bedspread I threw over myself when I tried to grab a night's sleep on the uncomfortable sofa: Violet

BUCKET TO GREECE (VOL. 6)

Burke's attempts to play the gracious hostess didn't extend to offering me the only bedroom. There was simply no escaping the suffocating smell, so omnipresent that it was easy to imagine the very wallpaper was stuck in place with chip grease rather than paste.

Whilst my mother was so accustomed to the smell she claimed to hardly notice it, it made me long for the fresh clean air of Meli with its familiar scents of honeysuckle and olive blossom, lemons and herbs. Instead of waking to the gentle tinkling of distant goats' bells I was rudely assailed by the din of refuse collectors dragging overflowing bins down the cobbled ginnel that ran down the back of the chippy. Deprived of my usual habit of sipping my first coffee on the balcony whilst appreciating the magnificent sea view, I resorted to throwing open the lounge window, only to be assaulted by the fetid stench of chips rising up from discarded newspaper wrappings littering the street.

"She said she'd rather be sent to the knacker's yard than an old folk's home," I told Milton.

"Violet is the independent type, I'm sure the council will find her a nice flat," Milton reassured me, clueless his words made me shudder.

V.D. BUCKET

In truth I dreaded the thought of my mother ending up in some high-rise flat on some rough council estate, too afraid of muggers to make her way to the shops. When I had shared my fears with Marigold she had scoffed unsympathetically, pointing out that Violet Burke is hardly some frail old lady and that she'd more than likely put the frighteners on any muggers. Nevertheless I remained uneasy, wondering how her swollen feet would manage the stairs in some imagined bleak high-rise block if the urine soaked lift was vandalised, or if she would feel isolated cast adrift from the chip shop regulars.

Such worries have made me consider the practicality of converting our downstairs storage into a granny flat so that Violet Burke could perhaps spend part of the year with us, without getting under our feet too much. To my surprise I have developed quite a liking for my mother, albeit in small doses; it rather crept up on me unawares. I made a mental note to get a sly quote for the necessary renovation work from Barry and Vangelis, without mentioning it to Marigold.

A granny flat would assure my mother her independence and allow her to escape the long dreary English winters confined in a high-rise, her feet too swollen to make it down the stairs to the nearest chippy. Admittedly I have no idea how Violet Burke would react to such an idea, nor have I broached the matter with Marigold; after all the demolition isn't a certainty yet and my imagination may be running away with me when I conjure up disgusting lodgings on a crime- ridden estate.

I reflected that my mother had begun to develop a few friendships in this area. She and our neighbour Kyria Maria spent hours talking at one another, rubbing along companionably despite their inability to understand the other's language. Vi gets on like a house on fire with the irrepressible Captain Vasos, and Panos is clearly taken with her. If she misses her old job at the chippy too much perhaps Nikos could take her on to fry chips and knock the place into spotless order. I'm sure Dina would be happy to hang up her mop.

"I can't believe a splendid woman like Violet hasn't been snapped up," Milton said for the umpteenth time. "Of course she isn't as handsome now as she was when she was younger, but she's certainly got a presence. I take it she's widowed."

"I'm sure my mother wouldn't appreciate

me gossiping about her personal life," I snapped, having no intention of airing Violet Burke's marital history in public. In truth I have no clue if she actually outlasted any of the four husbands she has mentioned, or indeed if the mentioned four represented the totally tally.

"Quite, wouldn't dream of gossiping about Violet, marvellous woman," Milton said, his lower lip visibly wobbling at his repeated failure to prise more personal information out of me about Vi.

"Well I must be getting on, I'm leading the Vathia excursion tomorrow," I said, hoping Milton would take the hint to clear off.

"I'll be on my way then...see you at the dinner party tomorrow evening."

Groaning inwardly at the reminder I waved him off and dug out my recipe for Greek fish soup, wondering if Marigold could successfully pass it off as French.

Chapter 4

*More Handsome
than the Prime Minister*

Marigold was sprawled out on the bed enjoying a late siesta, the new air conditioner blasting cold air and running up my electric bill. I noted with annoyance that Pickles was curled up on my pillow beside her; he is very fickle in his affections considering I am the one who indulges his extravagant taste for sardines. I doubted Pickles would be so keen to get up close and personal with

V.D. BUCKET

Marigold if he'd had the misfortune of suffering the inevitable consequences of tasting her foul cat paté. It could eat tinned cat food later and be grateful it had a lucky escape.

I decided to catch up with the news on television. Although Greek broadcasting tends to be a tad difficult to follow I do occasionally persevere in the hope of improving my language skills. The face of our new leader, Prime Minster Kostas Karamalis, flashed up on screen, New Democracy having defeated the previously reigning Pasok party back in the March elections. For the benefit of any readers that are interested in the inner workings of Greek politics, New Democracy is the nearest equivalent of the British Tories or the American Republicans, whilst Pasok has more socialist leanings, equating to the British Labour party or the American Democrats. A few of the villagers are vocal supporters of KKE, the Greek Communist party, and political arguments between different factions in the taverna tend to get quite robustly heated. Local political affiliations are mostly ingrained, voting patterns and party loyalty practically inherited family traits.

I must confess that my own particular musings about Kostas Karamalis lean to the shallow, centred on whether or not he is considered attractive. This preoccupation of mine was spawned through the rather useless phrase I had mastered during my initial attempts to memorise Greek that led to the misunderstanding that I had an unnatural interest in the Albanian Prime Minister Fatos Nano. I have turned the linguistic mix-up into an amusing anecdote in my book, admittedly exaggerating the details a tad with a touch of hyperbole for light relief; perhaps my particular brand of dry humour will appeal, though I'm sure it would be lost on the likes of Harold; my little quips always did go over his head.

I even sought out Marigold's opinion on the matter of Kostas Karamalis' attractiveness; she didn't hesitate to assure me that I am the more handsome as my wife considers the new prime minister to be a tad jowly with a receding hairline. She also says that he looks my age, even though he is twelve years younger. I reflected that he probably looks a bit knackered because he was pushing fifty when he fathered twins. The sleepless nights are already taking their toll on Barry's wrinkles and Cynthia only gave birth to one.

Unable to decipher the fast-paced spiel of

the four boxed talking-heads on screen, each shouting over the other, I turned the television off, deciding instead to catch up with the news online. For once there were no guests cluttering up the sofa-bed in my office so I was able to access the online Greek newspapers on my computer in peace. My frustration grew as I attempted to make sense of the words in the Euclidean alphabet and I opted instead for the translated version. As usual the English translation of the Greek news was a language botch-up. I scratched my head in quizzical fashion at the converted text that read 'the arrested man turned his knife on his wife and then at another woman, reportedly her boyfriend.' I wondered if the knife-toting criminal had stabbed his wife and her female friend, or his wife and her lover; or perchance his wife was a closet lesbian. Perhaps someone at the taverna could clarify the grisly details later.

A delightful image of a rich looking chocolate bundt cake caught my eye. Thinking Marigold may fancy baking one for the ex-pat dinner party I clicked on the recipe. Perusing the instructions I reflected Marigold would need a trip to a hardware store to get a grip on the cooking directions. Nevertheless I printed them off,

BUCKET TO GREECE (VOL. 6)

hoping my wife would derive some amusement if she attempted to follow them: 'In a large pan put two cans of olive oil soup and thoroughly slurry with the rod blender. Add the two yolks and mix with wire, pour there the mixture into a lubricate and flour medium-sized cake mold and bake for 50 minutes. To see if cake is bake dive into the center of a knife.'

Reflecting that I really needed to brush up on my Greek reading skills to avoid suffering such atrocious translations, I gave up and settled down to read the online Telegraph only to discover half their coverage was fixated on mind-numbingly boring football.

Marigold breezed into my office, desperate to impart the latest gossip from her friend Geraldine back in England. I exhaled in relief when my wife divulged that Geraldine had just telephoned, waking her from her siesta; at least I wasn't the one footing the bill for the long-distance call.

"Geraldine has a new boyfriend, it sounds like a good match as they are both scientists," Marigold announced.

"Since when did Geraldine give up taste testing pet food to become a scientist?" I asked.

"Oh Victor, must you always be so pedantic,

you know as well as I do that taste testing pet food requires a degree in food science..."

"Yes, but that doesn't entitle Geraldine to go around calling herself an actual scientist. Anyway what area of science does this new fellow dabble in?"

"He works with biological samples in a lab."

"Ah, that sounds interesting," I said, imagining something pioneering in gene analysis or vaccine development. "What area does he specialise in?"

"Sexually transmitted infections." At least Marigold had the grace to blush. "Apparently they are rife in Manchester now. It is such a relief that they are no longer referred to as venereal diseases. I know how keenly you feel the shame of your birth initials with their embarrassing connotations, but I expect that the youngsters of today wouldn't even make the connection. Anyway as I said to Geraldine, STI samples are a tad higher in the pecking order than stool samples, I'm sure if he analysed those for a living it would have been a deal breaker."

"And has Geraldine broken the news to Papas Andreas that she's walking out with another chap?" I asked.

BUCKET TO GREECE (VOL. 6)

"Not exactly, it's a difficult matter to broach, particularly with the language difficulty. Papas Andreas' telephone English is almost as abysmal as your telephone Greek."

"Well I hope she isn't expecting me to do her dirty work for her," I said. Geraldine had spent another week visiting us the previous September and had been quite indiscreet about her assignations with the local cleric, sneaking off to church with surprising regularity for an avowed agnostic.

"She is going to tell him, she has been ghosted too many times to inflict the same rude ending on someone else."

"Ghosted?"

"Oh do keep up Victor, it's the new way of dumping someone without bothering to tell them."

"It's not exactly the kind of information I need to keep abreast of, the last time I dumped a girl I was only just into long trousers," I said, blushing as I remembered the cripplingly embarrassing moment I had dreaded when I had to tell Belinda I didn't want to be her boyfriend anymore. I had worked myself into quite a lather, convinced I would break her heart, only to have my carefully rehearsed spiel met with complete indifference. The very next day the rejected Belinda was all over Derek Little like a rash, never so much as flinching as she got up close and personal with his rather virulent acne. "Anyway I do hope Geraldine lets the Papas down gently, it wouldn't do have our reputations tarnished by being associated with a heartless Jezebel."

"I'm sure his religion will offer him some comfort but it's not easy trying to maintain a long distance relationship, especially when nothing could ever have come from it," Marigold pointed out pragmatically. "Now, shall we walk over to the taverna for something to eat? Perhaps we could do a detour and call in on the baby; I haven't seen her for an absolute age."

"You were round there all morning. I rather fancy having you all to myself this evening." All the talk of ghosting had made me appreciate my loving relationship with Marigold; even during our occasional arguments she had never once resorted to dropping me without bothering to tell me.

Chapter 5

Spiros is Glum

Marigold linked my arm tightly as we strolled to the taverna, careful to avoid losing her footing on the potholed street. Sheer vanity prevented her from eschewing unsuitable footwear for something more practical; she refused to ditch her stylish heels for the Crocs that were becoming quite the unfashionable statement amongst the village women. In truth I was quite pleased that she insisted on maintaining her high standards; in a sleeveless lemon sundress paired with taupe heels, her Titian locks recently re-touched in Athena's kitchen, she looked quite the picture of loveliness. I hoped that my own drop in standards wouldn't embarrass her unduly; the late June evening was so hot that I had given into temptation and ventured out tieless, though I remained buttoned up to conceal any random grey chest hairs and I had given my leather sandals a good polishing.

Litsa came hobbling towards us clad in her usual black widow's weeds topped with a thick black cardigan, leaning heavily on her walking stick. A genuine smile softened her wrinkled features when she recognised us. "*Pou pas?*" I said by way of greeting, asking where she was going.

"*Sto spiti tou Barry. To ekana yia to moro, koita,*" she replied, telling us she was heading to Barry's house with a gift she had made for the baby. Delving into the Lidl carrier bag draped over one arm she produced a black hand-knitted bonnet topped with the most enormous yellow bobble, crafted in the style of a bee. The hat was duly followed by a matching black wool outfit resembling a sleeping bag, emblazoned with vibrant yellow stripes. "*I mikri Anastasia tha moiazei me melissa,*" Litsa said, declaring her unique creation would make little Anastasia look like a bee.

"*Einai omorfo*," Marigold gushed. As Litsa ambled away Marigold rolled her eyes, indicating she thought the baby gift was anything but beautiful. "What is this Greek obsession with wrapping babies up in thick woolly layers during the height of summer? And what on earth possessed Litsa to think that Cynthia would want to dress the baby in black?"

"She probably had a surplus of black wool left over from all those black cardies she knits," I guessed. "I'm not sure why the Greeks are so into swaddling, it definitely seems over the top in this heat."

"Cynthia is getting a bit tired of all the Greek ladies insisting Anastasia will catch a nasty chill unless every inch of her skin is wrapped up in multiple layers of something woolly," Marigold said despairingly. "They badger her terribly. I worry Cynthia is feeling a bit undermined by all the unwanted advice that contradicts her motherly instincts. The villagers are only happy if she has Anastasia swaddled up as tightly as an Egyptian mummy."

I shuddered at the thought. The heat really was too oppressive to imagine having all one's extremities encased in wool; it was bad enough that I had to wear socks in the summer to protect my ankles from blood-sucking mosquitoes, but at least they were made from a light cotton blend and spared my feet from close contact with the inevitable layer of grimy dust on the taverna floor. The ladies of Meli had been so busy with their knitting needles that Cynthia had enough baby outfits and blankets to open a shop. Although some of the creations were, to put it bluntly, quite hideous, I couldn't fault the generosity of the well-meaning villagers.

Arriving at the taverna we were surprised to discover the outside seating area practically overflowing with people we didn't recognise. The only free table was the one we usually made a point of avoiding since it was in the direct path of the thick smoke wafting over from Nikos' grill.

"You grab the table whilst I pop inside to say hello to Dina," I said. It was more than my life was worth to not stop in to greet Dina who treated me like an honorary son. Stepping into the empty taverna I noticed that some of the usual tables were missing, having no doubt been dragged outside to accommodate the excess of patrons. Making my way towards the kitchen I sidestepped the pushchair containing Nikoleta, noticing the baby born on the day of Barry's wedding was wrapped up in enough layers to ward off the freeze of a Siberian winter. Her chubby little mittened hands moved to instinctively swat away a random fly, while her bootied feet tried to kick off the blankets. A single curl escaped her woolly bonnet, resting damply on a flushed cheek. Nikoleta gurgled in delight when I yanked the blanket to one side and passed her the cuddly toy she'd lobbed on the floor. Dina immediately rushed over to tuck the blanket firmly back into place, tutting with displeasure at my impudence in daring to uncover the infant.

Dina was too busy to stop more than momentarily. Up to her neck in salads and chips she told me that the place was packed out because many Athenians had descended on their ancestral homes in the area for the weekend.

"Ela Victor, parte to psomi," she instructed, gathering me up in a motherly embrace before piling me high with baskets of bread to take outside. Not bothering to remind her I no longer worked there I accepted the baskets, passing them to Eleni to distribute amongst the tables as I ran into her in the doorway. Joining Marigold

I couldn't help but notice that the Athenians were nowhere near as laid back as the locals, impatiently shouting across at Eleni to bring them more wine before she'd even had chance to unload the bread baskets. Unusually Kostis had been roped in to help out, hurrying to comply with his father's demand to bring another table outside when some of the local elderly men turned up, visibly annoyed that their usual table was occupied.

Nikos left the grill to come across and greet us, complaining "some the one has been telling the food here is the best."

"Well that's certainly true," I agreed.

"But I not like to have all these foreigns to know it," he replied, wiping the sweat from his brow with a tea towel. His words made me smile, even as I winced at his unhygienic disregard for the tea towel. Nikos preferred to run the taverna as a meeting spot for the locals rather than be run off his feet catering to tourists. Whilst technically I was a foreigner in Greece, I was now accepted as a local in Meli; ironically it was the Greeks that hailed from Athens that Nikos considered as foreign tourists.

Spiros arrived, his unshaven face looking glum. Although I had envisaged a quiet evening alone with Marigold I didn't hesitate to beckon him to join us rather than see him relegated to the table of garlic chomping pensioners.

"Did you manage to get hold of Sampaguita?" I asked in genuine concern.

Grabbing a toothpick and making mindless stabs at the paper tablecloth, Spiros sighed heavily. "She do nothing but the cry. She feel too much the guilt. I tell her it is not her fault, but still she weep."

"Do you think it would help if I perhaps telephoned her and try to make her see reason? Sometimes a woman to woman chat can be helpful," Marigold said, placing a hand on Spiros' arm sympathetically. I flinched at the prospect of Marigold running up my telephone bill by making long-distance calls to the Philippines, before relaxing. An exorbitant phone bill was a small price to pay if there was any chance of reuniting Spiros and Sampaguita. Spiros' happiness depended on it.

A sparkle I hadn't seen for a while returned to the undertaker's eyes. "You would do that for me, Marigold?"

"Of course, what happened was just one of those things and Sampaguita mustn't blame herself. If she hadn't cared so much for Leo she wouldn't feel so bad."

"Marigold blamed herself every time we lost Aunty Beryl, but short of handcuffing the old lady to the bed there is nothing she could have done to prevent her from wandering off on occasion," I said.

During an exceptionally cold wet spell in February Sampaguita had risen before daylight to discover the back door ajar and Leo's bed empty. With no way of knowing how long the Alzheimer suffering pensioner had been on the loose, Sampaguita rushed outside to try and locate him. Unable to find him she telephoned Spiros who immediately roused the villagers and organised a search party. It was still dark when I received the call to join the search. Our torches were long extinguished, no longer necessary in the dull grey light of the dreary wet day, when Panos eventually came across the practically comatose body of Leo stretched out under an olive tree in one of his fields. Poor Leo was clad in nothing but pyjamas and slippers, soaked through from the rain. Spiros wrapped his shivering body in blankets and loaded him into the back of the hearse, recklessly disregarding the speed limit in his mad dash to get his uncle to the hospital.

BUCKET TO GREECE (VOL. 6)

Despite receiving the very best medical care, Leo unfortunately passed away, never recovering from the pneumonia he succumbed to on the fateful night he went missing. Sampaguita stayed by his bedside faithfully for the three-weeks he was hospitalised, blaming herself constantly in spite of Spiros' assurance that it wasn't her fault.

Casting my mind back I recalled Spiros calling in at the house the day before his Uncle Leo went missing. Spiros told me he needed a favour, his excitement palpable when he asked if I would babysit Leo on Saturday evening so that he could take his fragrant Filipana flower out for a romantic meal and pop the question. "I think she say yes Victor," Spiros said, revealing the gaudy diamond engagement ring he had purchased. Unfortunately the lovebirds spent their Saturday night by Leo's hospital bedside, romance the last thing on their minds.

After the funeral Sampaguita remained inconsolable. Spiros, sensitive enough to realise that the timing wasn't right for a marriage proposal, persuaded Sampaguita that a visit home to spend time with her children in the Philippines might make her feel better, a move he now bitterly regretted.

"Without the uncle to take the care of the Sampaguita not see how she can to return to the village, she say if she return to the *Ellada* she must to find the new job in the Athens," Spiros confided. "I tell her she can to live in the uncle's house, but she say it will to make her the burden. You think I should to propose the marriage down the telephone?"

"Let me try speaking to her tomorrow Spiro, she may find a telephone proposal overwhelming," Marigold said. "I think the best thing to do is to convince her to return to Meli so that you can reignite your relationship naturally, without her feeling pressured."

"This is the good idea Marigold, not to put the pressure on the Sampaguita. But how to convince her to return without the local work?"

"We must find her some work in the area to make her feel indispensible. Cynthia is really going to need a hand with the baby now that she's returning to work part-time and I'm sure she'd be happy to leave her with Sampaguita. We just need to find someone else who needs a hand around the house, if Sampaguita feels needed she'll settle back more readily."

"Marigold, I could to kiss you," Spiros declared, planting a smacker on my wife's forehead. His previous glumness was replaced with a new enthusiasm as he called across to Nikos to throw an extra portion of chicken on the grill. He had been so down in the doldrums since Sampaguita left that his appetite had suffered, but now, with fresh hope, he appeared hungry for food once again.

The difficult time he had suffered had naturally been compounded by burying his third and final uncle, his last immediate family member. For once he appeared to be in no hurry to flog off the house he had inherited, hoping that Sampaguita would agree to stay there if she returned to Meli.

Chapter 6

Stomping the Grapes

"Oh look, it's that handsome bee fellow." A sharp nudge in my side accompanied Marigold's words, causing my wine to slop out of my glass. I sighed in irritation as the wine soaked through my shirt, leaving a sticky damp residue on my chest hairs. Watching the stain blossom I had an almost visceral flashback; it reminded me of the juices seeping from the grapes when I'd given Nikos a hand, or should I say foot, with the wine making the previous September.

BUCKET TO GREECE (VOL. 6)

Although Nikos only grows grapes for eating rather than wine making, each harvest he buys a sufficiency of grapes from an organic vineyard in the Peloponnese to produce enough *spitiko krasi* to meet the taverna's annual needs. Nikos is of course a great believer in the traditional method of making wine by stomping the grapes by foot, *sfragizontas ta stafylia* in Greek, rather than with more modern mechanical methods. He has never invested in the necessary machinery, preferring instead to rope in free labour by talking up the ancient practice of pigeage as an authentic Greek experience.

I must confess to having my doubts on several scores. Nikos had roped me into helping out with the traditional bread making by convincing me it was a similar authentic Greek experience, failing to warn me it was back breaking work involving hours of kneading dough into loaves to be baked in a primitive twig-fired outside oven. Nikos scoffed at my concern, telling me that although the ancient Greeks got their servants to do the actual grape stomping he didn't consider me a servant, but a good friend. "You will to let down the hair and enjoy it Victor, I promise to you."

My other reservation concerned the sanitary

nature of bare feet coming into such close proximity to the end product. Nikos laughed off my concerns, assuring me the practice was blessed by Dionysus, the Greek god of wine. He said that Hippocrates would hardly have extolled the virtue of wine made by such a method, prescribing it not only as a medicine but as a powerful antiseptic, if it wasn't germ free. "When the juice erupt from the grape it make the alcohol that murder the bacteria," Nikos claimed with authority. Considering the spit and sawdust state of the taverna I was inclined to be sceptical about anything Nikos had to say on the subject of bacteria, though I must confess in almost two years of eating there I have never come down with food poisoning despite Dina's very casual approach to cleaning.

Reminding me how much I loved his wine Nikos explained that squashing the grapes by foot speeded up the fermentation process, giving his *spitiko* that special kick. Determined to have me participate in the stomping he appealed to my interest in history by lamenting it was a pity that the ancient terracotta amphorae used to store wine had been replaced with plastic bottles. It wasn't too difficult for Nikos to wear down my resistance; apart from my odd reservation I did rather fancy trying it out and sinking my bare feet into a bucket of plump sun-ripened grapes.

Nikos further suckered me in by outlining the special sanitary practices he insisted his grape stompers adhere to. Falling for his duplicitous falsehoods I duly shaved every hair off my legs below the knee and wrapped one of Marigold's scarves around my head to prevent any stray hairs contaminating the wine as per Nikos' instructions, even though the headscarf rather contradicted Nikos' promise that I could let my hair down. Feeling decidedly self-conscious in a woman's headscarf I reminded my wife she had been a tad hasty in insisting I bin the practical hair nets I had used in my days as a public health inspector.

Greek music blasted out as I helped Marigold to step into a wooden barrel. Taking my place in the adjacent barrel I felt the unusual texture of the cold grapes beneath my skin creating an odd squishy sensation. In no time at all I was stomping along to the music, my feet growing ever stickier as the juices were crushed from the increasingly pulpy fruit. Marigold's laughter was infectious as she tramped the grapes whilst swaying along to the music, soliciting indulgent smiles from Dina who was almost up to her knees in mulched fruit. "*Argotera kano dolmades apo ta fylla,*" Dina called over, promising to make *dolmades* from the leaves later.

Whilst he stamped his feet in a nearby barrel Nikos kept us entertained by doling out snippets of history pertaining to wine and the ancients. "Victor you know the ancient Greeks dilute the wine with the water or the honey to avoid getting the drunken."

"I remember reading that drunkenness was rather frowned on at ancient symposiums," I called over, wondering why Nikos had neglected to wear a head scarf. "I think it was the fourth century poet Amphis who extolled the virtue of boiled cabbage as an effective hangover cure if there was any overindulgence." The fact had stuck in my mind because I found it amusing, making me think that Harold could have saved a small fortune on Alka Seltzer if only he'd followed the time-honoured boiled cabbage remedy.

Stomping proved to be hot work in the sun. I dabbed at my forehead with Marigold's headscarf to prevent the perspiration from dripping into the juices. Noticing I was getting a tad overheated Nikos called out "I bring you the water," before climbing out of his barrel and marching off through the field on grape stained feet. I shuddered squeamishly when after returning with the bottled water Nikos jumped right back into the barrel without bothering to rinse his feet. Noticing that Nikos' legs below his rolled up trouser cuffs were completely hairy I wondered if I'd perhaps misunderstood him when he'd told me I needed to shave mine. Giving him the benefit of the doubt I put it down to yet another language mix up; that is until Panos turned up.

The welly wearing farmer marched over to the side of my barrel and peering at my legs he doubled over in laughter. Finally catching his breath Panos shouted over to Nikos "*To ekana, xifise ta podia tou, sas chrostao pente evro.*" My temper momentarily flared when I comprehended that Panos had said 'he did it, he shaved his legs, I owe you five euros,' and it dawned on me that I had been well and truly duped into removing my leg hair for a bet. I couldn't stay cross for long, joining in the laughter when Nikos adopted a mincing pose before calling back "*To derma tou einai toso omalo tora.*" It was true after all; my depilated skin really was exceptionally smooth now.

V.D. BUCKET

When the familiar figure of Guzim appeared Nikos instructed Panos to give the five euros he'd won directly to the Albanian since he'd agreed to pay him the paltry sum for helping out for an hour or two. I winced in horror as Guzim removed his flip flops, exposing grimy feet with flaking skin and a suspiciously yellow elongated toe nail. Before I could voice my objection to the disgusting state of his feet Guzim jumped straight into a barrel, most likely contaminating the wine with some nasty infection he'd picked up from his pet rabbit.

Needless to say I couldn't stomach the thought of a glass of *spitiko* for many months after witnessing Guzim's foul feet in direct contact with the grapes. Not wishing to hurt Nikos' feelings by disparaging his truly excellent *spitiko* I pretended I'd developed a taste for beer, ordering a bottle of Amstel whenever I was in the taverna. I continued to enjoy a glass of wine at home if it came from a glass bottle, confident that more rigorous standards would apply to the production of shop bought wine undergoing quality control, though I must confess that shop bought plonk didn't taste half as good as Nikos' liquid nectar.

I have never really acquired a taste for beer,

finding it terribly gassy, but I preserved with the bottled brew until Marigold pointed out that I was beginning to develop a beer belly. One evening Vangelis poured me a glass of *spitiko* in the taverna and I guzzled it down without thinking or associating it with Guzim's feet. Immediately an explosion of exquisite flavours reminded me of what I'd been missing and I've been hooked on *spitiko* again ever since. Pragmatically I disassociate Guzim's feet from the end product in the same manner in which I overcame my repugnance of slime when enjoying a dish of freshly caught snails.

I didn't fall for all of Nikos' wine related tall stories. After telling me about an ancient Greek ritual where the men would don women's clothing and run between temples whilst holding bunches of grapes to celebrate the end of the grape harvest, Nikos assured me that this tradition was still enacted annually in the village. His attempts to persuade me to wear one of Marigold's dresses to participate in this ancient tradition fell flat because I couldn't squeeze myself into any of my wife's dresses. Of course there was no such village ritual, but I never let on that if only my figure had been a tad slighter Nikos may have got another one over on me and made me the laughing stock of the village.

Another sharp nudge from Marigold woke me from my reverie. Looking up I spotted Giannis and his supermodel girlfriend standing awkwardly near the grill, disappointment etched on their faces when they realised there were no free tables. "Shall we invite them to join us?"

"Of course, the more the merrier," I agreed, frantically dabbing the spilt wine from my shirt with a paper napkin. Since Spiros' presence meant that Marigold and I would not be enjoying the romantic dinner for two I had envisaged, another couple at the table wouldn't make any difference.

Giannis and his supermodel girlfriend eagerly accepted Spiros' invitation to join us, Giannis introducing his girlfriend as Poppy and telling us she came from the coastal village that housed the *Dimarcheio*. Up close Poppy was even lovelier than she'd appeared when I'd seen her riding pillion on Giannis' motorbike, her willowy figure nicely set off in a casual crop top and jeans. They certainly made a handsome couple, Giannis with his toned and muscled physique and unruly dark locks, Poppy with her flowing raven hair, high cheekbones and striking black eyebrows. When I commented that I didn't know that Poppy was a Greek name Spiros enlightened me that Poppy was the informal usage of Kalliope.

"It is so very kind of you to invite us to join you," Poppy said in perfect English with the merest hint of an accent. I presumed she must have picked up the language through her jet-setting lifestyle of international travel. "Giannis' mama went over to Nektar to care for his grandfather who is sick and she has not returned yet. There was nothing to eat in the house." Immediately switching to Greek she repeated her words for Giannis' benefit since he doesn't speak English.

"*Tipota, den einai kati yia fagito,*" Giannis said, confirming there was no food to be had in his mother's kitchen.

"I help the Ioanna with the many bag of the shopping this morning," Spiros contradicted, his bushy eyebrows furrowed in puzzlement, referring to Giannis' mother and speaking English for our benefit, before turning his attention to Giannis. Whilst the two Greek men chatted together in their own language I continued my conversation with Poppy.

"Yes, there is plenty of food in the kitchen but neither Giannis nor I have a clue how to cook it. I can barely boil water without burning it," Poppy admitted with a tinkling laugh.

"I thought that every Greek girl was taught to cook almost before she can walk," Marigold exclaimed in surprise.

"My parents forbid me from taking the time away from my lessons," Poppy replied. "They always stressed the importance of a good education above all else and encouraged me to concentrate on my studies. Mama is such a good cook she spoils me."

"Well it's certainly paid off in your impeccable mastery of the English language," I noted, wondering just how much education it required to be a supermodel. Perhaps there was more to the job than simply dressing up to pose and pout in front of a camera. The way in which Poppy was tucking into Dina's chips with obvious relish made me reassess my impression that models subsisted on nothing but diet coke and celery. "I expect your English comes in useful with all the international travel you must do."

Poppy threw her head back and laughed. "I sometimes struggle to understand the native accent in the city I work in, the dialect is not always easy to decipher, though it does have an attractive lilt."

BUCKET TO GREECE (VOL. 6)

"So you're primarily based in one city?" I asked, wondering if it was perhaps Paris, Milan or New York.

"Yes Edinburgh, the Laboratory for Bacterial Evolution and Pathogenesis is located at the University there."

"Bacterial evolution," I parroted in confusion, thinking the laboratory an unlikely place to host a fashion runway.

"I specialise in Streptococci for my PhD studies. I appreciate it can sound like a bit of a mouthful to the uninitiated layman."

"But I had it on good authority you are a supermodel," I stuttered in confusion. "Do you combine modelling with academia?"

"What good authority?" Marigold interrupted.

"Barry told me, I think he got it from Vangelis…"

"The pair of them are worse gossips than some of the old dears in the village," Marigold said to Poppy, sending a withering look in my direction. "They simply assume a woman with a pretty face doesn't have a brain."

"I assumed no such thing, as I said I had it on good authority that Poppy is a supermodel," I objected. "So you study Streptococci, now that is a bacterium that I find truly fascinating."

"You have heard of it?" Poppy asked, her turn to be surprised.

"Naturally I came across it during my illustrious career as a public health inspector. Are you studying to enter a similar field?" I asked, delighted to find someone who shared my interest in germs.

"My focus is on the detrimental effect of Streptococci on the endocardium following bacterial colonisation. You are familiar with the research Victor?"

"Victor's expertise is really in insanitary food practices..." Marigold interrupted.

"I'm up to date enough with the jargon to understand you wouldn't want someone with a streptococcal infected open wound preparing your food..."

Spiros interrupted me before I could continue, perhaps just as well since I was floundering out of my depth when it came to specialist research into infective endocarditis. It could be a tad embarrassing to be exposed as having less expertise in bacteria than a mere slip of a girl in her twenties.

"The Giannis say the grandfather is the sick and refuse to move in with the daughter Ioanna.

BUCKET TO GREECE (VOL. 6)

She is the worn out running to look after him in the Nektar and she neglect the son," Spiros said. "The Giannis say the Ioanna need help, I think the Sampaguita could to care for the grandfather. Marigold, you tell this to the Sampaguita on the telephone, tell to her the grandfather need her help."

"It certainly sounds like a solution that would help everyone, it must be terrible for Giannis not having his mother at his beck and call to cook for him," Marigold said.

Her obvious sarcasm clearly went way over Spiros' head since he responded, "It is not just the cooking she neglect, the Giannis not know how to use the washing machine or the iron, or make the bed."

Rolling her eyes at me Marigold bit her tongue, choosing to keep her own counsel. The local habit of grown men having their mothers run round after them, catering to their every whim, was one that left us perplexed. We had brought Benjamin up to be independent, perfectly capable of getting to grips with cooking and cleaning, but here in Greece there were men in their thirties and forties who acted like overgrown toddlers, still relying on their mothers to do everything for them.

V.D. BUCKET

At some point many men cut the apron strings by taking a wife, expecting the new spouse to immediately assume the domestic duties to the same standards set by their over indulgent mothers. In many instances the new wife ends up saddled with running around after the new mother-in-law, the latter often taking advantage by downing tools, putting her feet up and barking orders. A prime example of a victim of this custom is Eleni; in addition to tending the baby she is at the beck and call of her husband Kostis as well as being expected to help out in the taverna. Fortunately for Eleni, although she has her hands full, Dina doesn't take advantage by sitting around and barking out orders. Even though Kostis is married, Dina always drops everything to ensure the idle son she dotes on is duly mollycoddled.

Since Giannis had lived independently in a city before returning to live with his mother in Meli I hazarded a guess that he was pulling a fast one by claiming to be so helpless. It struck me that Poppy was too intelligent to be as domestically clueless as she made out; no doubt she was simply not prepared to be taken advantage of by her boyfriend.

My ruminations were interrupted by the

BUCKET TO GREECE (VOL. 6)

Athenians becoming rowdy, shouting over to Nikos *"Ferte tin tileorasi, theloume to podosfairo."* I groaned inwardly as they demanded that Nikos bring the television because they wanted to watch the football: I always make a point of avoiding any establishments that subject their clientele to a television blaring out. The Athenians insistence on catching the match became more vehement until Nikos gave in, instructing Kostis to bring the television set down from the apartment upstairs. Like me Nikos was no fan of televised events being shown in the taverna; the last time the television had made an appearance was when Dimitris took the hot seat on 'Who Wants to be a Millionaire.' Catching my eye Nikos apologised, saying "What can I to do Victor, the Greece is playing?"

Before I could object, my mobile rang. It was Barry demanding to know where I was and threatening to do vile things to Mrs Trout unless I could offer him a bolt hole to escape from his mother-in-law. I told him to come and join us in the taverna, warning him that it might get a tad noisy since Nikos had agreed to screen the football. "In that case I'll bring Lester along with me. Anne is refusing to allow him to watch the football here," Barry said.

Chapter 7

A Football Flutter

By the time Barry and his father-in-law Lester turned up Kostis had dumped the television set on the outside wall, an extension lead stretching precariously through an open window and across the outside seating area, presenting a dangerous trip hazard. Whilst I was very tempted to strenuously object to this blatant violation of health and safety regulations, I didn't fancy a confrontation with the by-now well lubricated Athenians. Considering the state of a couple of them I felt sorely tempted to recommend an early morning portion of boiled cabbage as an effective hangover cure.

The Athenians were in the throes of a cumulative hissy fit over the screen showing nothing but rotating static lines instead of a picture. Kostis gave the set a few thumps, a futile gesture which did nothing to fix the problem. Nikos, holding the barbecue tongs in a threatening gesture to keep the football crazed visitors at bay practically pounced on Barry the moment he walked in, begging him, "Barry, you must to make the television work."

"No problem," Barry obligingly agreed, fiddling around with the decrepit wires. Shouts of *'Bravo'* filled the air when Barry managed to get the television to project a clear picture just as the quarter-final of the UEFA match kicked off. We all budged up so that Barry and Lester could squash in beside us, some judicious swapping of seats allowing Spiros, Giannis, Poppy and Lester a view of the game, the rest of us patently disinterested.

"I'm sorry darling, this isn't exactly the quiet evening together I envisaged," I said to Marigold.

"It is hardly your fault that the place has been

invaded by football fanatics," Marigold said, squeezing my hand. "It is almost worth putting up with the football in order to enjoy Nikos' chicken. Anyway the Athenians seem to be settling down now that the television is on."

Marigold made a valid point. In comparison to the antics of football hooligans I had seen portrayed on the news, the Greek football fans were now sedately glued to the screen. I supposed I could excuse a bit of noisy exuberance considering their national team was playing and one should perhaps expect a display of patriotic pride on such an occasion.

"No doubt you will be supporting England tonight," I said in an effort to make small-talk with Lester.

Turning away from the screen Lester gave me an odd look, conveying the impression I was an irritant that needed putting in its place. "England isn't playing, it's France against Greece," he said in a condescending tone, his right eye frantically twitching.

"Oh, Barry said you were keen to see the match so I automatically presumed England must be playing," I said, a tad taken aback by his disdainful manner. When we had previously met Lester had struck me as the obsequious type, but perchance he dropped his toadying mien when his wife let him off her leash.

"So who do you think will win?" Although I was not in the slightest bit interested in his reply I decided to persevere in an attempt to engage him in polite conversation; after all we were loosely related. Giving him the benefit of the doubt I didn't discount the possibility that his involuntary twitch spawned his cantankerous attitude.

"Well the Frenchies will win, obviously. I'd love to see them get their comeuppance, but the Greeks have no form. It's a miracle that bunch of amateurs made it this far," Lester said in a contemptuous tone. I was surprised to discover that without his wife speaking over him, Lester actually had a voice, even though his conversational skills were less impressive than those of our cats

"Victor knows nothing about football, he's just making conversation," Barry interrupted, his eyes pleading with me not to rise to Lester's bait. "Personally I'm rooting for Greece; I've got money riding on them. Even though I'm not that into footie I put a tenner on Greece winning the championship. Vangelis was egging me on to match his bet, and the odds were 80 to 1."

V.D. BUCKET

"That would be an excellent return..." I began to say until I was rudely interrupted by Lester.

"Well that's a tenner down the drain and no mistake," he scoffed, his twitch out of control. "I'm not sure that Anne would approve of you frittering away good money on gambling. I wouldn't like to be in your shoes when she finds out."

"I fail to see what Barry chooses to do with his money is any business of your wife," I said, flabbergasted by his remark.

"Well it is her business if Barry is expecting Cynthia to go back to work to keep him in betting money."

"Barry is not one to gamble, but if he fancied a flutter on our national team it is quite understandable," I snapped, appalled by Lester's rudeness. Fortunately he turned his back on me to concentrate on the game before further words could be exchanged.

"Lester is football crazy but his selfish wife flatly refused to let him watch it at home," Barry hissed in my ear.

"Well you're the man of the house, you should have stood up to her," I said.

"Not likely," Barry groaned. "I'm not getting

in the middle of a domestic. Once we'd got Anastasia settled all I fancied was a quiet evening in snuggling up with Cynthia on the couch and reigniting the romantic spark. Fat chance of that though when my mother-in-law plonked herself down in the middle of us and all hell broke loose over the remote control."

"Perhaps you'll have better luck tomorrow evening; you'll finally have the place to yourselves if you can come up with an excuse to get out of the monthly meeting of the ex-pat dining club. Marigold is planning to invite the Trouts; she hasn't experienced the sharp end of Lester's snide tongue yet."

"Lester never has a word to say for himself when Anne is around. I expect Cyn will be exhausted tomorrow night after her first day back at work," Barry said glumly. "Having that pair cramping my style has really made me appreciate how lucky I am having you as a brother in-law, not all in-laws are so easy to get along with."

Pleased by his compliment, I responded with a statement of fact. "Come now Barry, you have always appreciated me."

Marigold gave me another sharp nudge in the side. Leaning in closely she whispered "that chap over there keeps staring at me, I find it rather unnerving." Since my wife was sitting next to the ravishing Poppy I presumed any drooling stares would be directed at the younger woman and Marigold was simply indulging in a vain fit of false flattery. Looking across I caught the eye of an Athenian man sending daggers drawn looks at my wife, rather than the impassioned glances of admiration she had imagined. *"Peite tis na kinithei, blokarei to pofasfairo,"* he shouted over, none too politely demanding I tell Marigold to move as she was blocking his view of the football.

Further attempts at conversation were drowned out by the Athenians keeping up an over excited commentary on the game. Even the local old-timers appeared engrossed in the match, their shouts of encouragement joining forces with those of the Athenians as they yelled out *"na ton antimetopisei,"* tackle him, *"pigainete sti gonia,"* take it to the corner, and *"ela"* come on. Thinking to improve my Greek I asked Spiros what Zagorakis meant when I heard it called out repeatedly. "Victor, you have no the idea of the footballing, the Zagorakis is the name of the player who captain the team."

Spiros was quite correct; I was not only disinterested but completely clueless. It was quite beyond me how the fans could possibly identify which member of the team had his foot on the ball when they were all running at speed whilst kitted out in identical white and blue uniforms.

Dina came out of the taverna carrying platters of chips and promptly tripped over the electrical lead running from the television, disconnecting the picture and sending chips flying everywhere. The air was filled with more than just chips when the Greek fans let loose with some foul language which Barry was forced to translate for my benefit, being more familiar with foreign expletives due to his quick mastery of builder's Greek. I blushed, thinking that Poppy was too young to be exposed to such coarse obscenities, until I realised she was joining in, equally irate that Dina's clumsy footing had caused the screen to go blank. Fortunately Barry soon had the television restored to full working order and excited calls of "*Ela* Angelo" and "*Ela* Lakis" resumed.

Litsa's appearance triggered cries of "Proseche" meaning be careful, as the black clad widow hobbled towards the exposed extension lead. Fortunately she narrowly avoided tripping over the wire and becoming a cropper, but the screen went dead when her walking stick caught the electrical lead and the attached plug was yanked from its socket. The resultant expletives were much too colourful to repeat, but luckily the picture was almost instantly restored when Kostis stuck the plug back in the indoor socket. Litsa shuffled over to her brother Mathias, dutifully delivering his regular evening dose of a garlic clove. I was touched that although he had seemed preoccupied by the match he took the time to pull out a chair and pour her a glass of *spitiko*. They appeared to have developed a new closeness since her spell in the hospital.

There was a collective scream of delight at the sixty-five-minute mark when Angelos Charisteas headed a goal into the opposing net, or so Spiros informed me. Presuming it meant the end of the interminable game I duly joined in with a few cries of *"Bravo Ellada,"* surprised when Spiros told me it wasn't actually over yet. However the French team were no match for the superior Greeks who soared on to a victorious win, having scored the only goal in the game.

Worried that the victory may descend into scenes such as those I had seen on the television when football hooligans rampaged through the streets, the actual win was celebrated in a very decorous fashion, with cries of Bravo and rounds of applause celebrating the national team qualifying to progress to the semi-final. Despite my complete indifference to the game the mood was infectious and I felt a real sense of pride in this Hellenic achievement which meant so much to the natives of my adopted country. The prevailing mood appeared to be one of elated shock that Greece had made it to the semi-final, and I supposed it was simply national pride that made my fellow taverna goers think that Greece would win the whole shebang and walk off with the 2004 UEFA cup.

"It seems that your little flutter paid off," I said to Barry.

"Not quite yet, Greece needs to win the semi-final and the final before I can cash in."

"Is that likely?"

"You must be joking, the Greek win tonight was nothing more than a lucky fluke," Lester interrupted, only to be put in his place by Spiros declaring, "Our Greek heroes live up to the slogan on the team bus: *I Archaia Ellada eiche 12 theous. I synchroni Ellada echei 11.*"

"Something about gods?" Marigold asked quizzically.

"The Ancient Greece has the 12 gods, the modern Greece has the 11," Spiros translated helpfully, his voice bursting with pride.

All the clapping and cheering disturbed Nikoleta who had been dozing indoors. Dina carried her granddaughter outside so that we could all duly coo over the baby. One of the Athenians instigated a quick whip round, presenting the proceeds to Dina with instructions to treat Nikoleta to something nice, seemingly considering the cute infant a lucky mascot for the national team. It was touching how the Greeks always made such a complete fuss of babies. I made a mental note to reduce Cynthia's load by offering to take Anastasia out; she was sure to be greeted rapturously if I brought her along to the taverna.

Since I had an early start the next morning with the Vathia tour we decided to make a move and head home. As we bid our goodbyes Apostolos, the local barber, surprised us with an invitation to attend a party at his home the following week to celebrate his name day. It was unusual to receive invitations to local homes unless they were extended by close friends because most of the Greeks we knew tended to gather in tavernas for any celebrations, so we accepted eagerly.

"I do hope that you won't feel obligated to let him cut your hair after attending his party," Marigold said as we walked home in the moonlight. "I really don't think you'd suit a lop-sided neckline darling."

Chapter 8

A Garden Intruder

As we reached our gate Marigold rushed indoors in desperate need of the bathroom; as always she had made a point of avoiding the facilities in the local taverna in case Dina hadn't been round with the bleach. Barry told Lester to head home without him, saying we had some important business to attend to. Certain that Lester would pass some kind of judgemental comment if we revealed that our important business involved dragging Harold's old bathtub out of storage and secreting it behind the new grape arbor, we didn't bother to fill Lester in on the details.

"It must be some kind of shady racket you've got going on at this time of night," Lester observed; I would have sworn his twitch was going into overdrive if it wasn't too dark to get a clear view. "I'm beginning to have my doubts if you are a suitable husband Barry, first it's your gambling problem and now these nefarious late night dealings."

"It's barely gone 10.30 and Barry doesn't have a gambling problem," I snapped. "If you must know Barry is simply giving me a hand to move an awkward and heavy piece of furniture that I can't manage to shift on my own. Feel free to lend a hand dragging the unwieldy item if you like Lester."

"I'll pass; Anne will already be thinking the worst as we've stayed out so late," he replied. Stalking off in the dark he threw a final warning over his shoulder. "Don't be too long Barry or Anne will expect a proper explanation from you."

"I can see why my sofa-bed is beginning to look so attractive," I said to Barry. "Your father-in-law is unspeakably vile. I'm certainly not used to being spoken down to by a man who stands a head shorter than me. Do you suppose that Cynthia was abandoned at birth and adopted by that dreadful pair?"

"Afraid there were no reports of buckets left at railway stations…to think I thought you had it bad with Violet Burke, she's a positive pussy cat compared to Cynthia's parents. The funny thing is that Lester appeared normal until this evening, he never says boo to a goose when he's with Anne. I'd never have guessed he had a mind of his own, and not a pleasant one at that," Barry sighed.

"It strikes me that she must stifle his natural dictatorial tendencies," I said. "Well at least you can wangle the night off from them tomorrow if you can come up with an excuse to avoid the dinner party, but after that we need to come up with a plan to get shut of them. Do you foresee any objections from Cynthia?"

"No, I think she'd be happy to be rid; they're sucking the life out of her and they don't offer any practical help with Anastasia. Come on, let's check the coast is clear before we drag the bath outside."

Making our way into the garden Barry gripped my arm to stall my progress, pointing towards something lurking by the side of the vegetable patch. The darkness made it impossible to make out if the shape was an animal or something more sinister, though images of recalcitrant sheep and goats flashed through my mind. As my eyes adjusted to the blackness I discerned it was a figure, a deduction echoed by Barry hissing in my ear "It looks like a kneeling figure. Look, I'm pretty sure that's a backside pointing upwards. Do you suppose it's praying?"

"Not likely, it's Guzim and as far as I know he's a heathen," I hissed back, recognising the slight shabby figure of the Albanian shed dweller. I couldn't imagine why he was creeping around the vegetable patch in the dark since he was free to help himself to any surplus veggies as part of his gardening perks.

"*Guzim, ti kaneis sto edafos?*" I called out, asking him what he was doing on the ground. At the sound of my voice Guzim shot upright, clutching his chest in an exaggerated fashion as though suffering a heart attack.

"*Me fovasai, ti kaneis edo?*" Guzim shouted, saying I had frightened him and asking what I was doing there.

"*Einai o kipos mou,*" I answered, pointing out that it was my garden. Surely I didn't owe

Guzim an explanation regarding my nocturnal presence on my own land; after all he was the creeping interloper. I asked him again what he was doing there, but instead of replying Guzim indicated I should shush before once again prostrating himself on the ground. Barry and I stood around like a couple of spare parts, at a loss as to what Guzim was up to.

My ears pricked up as a loud rustling noise emanated from the vegetable patch, sounding rather ominous in the brooding silence of the night. I made a hasty exploratory search of my pockets, trying to locate the torch I usually carried, just as Guzim hurled himself forward, landing face first in my carefully cultivated lettuces. As he sprang to his feet I finally located the elusive torch, its full beam revealing Guzim holding aloft an unidentifiable object, his face suffused in a toothless grin of triumph, a lettuce leaf limply dangling over one ear.

"*Echete syntagi yia soupa helonas?*" Guzim called out, his words so clearly distinct rather than mumbled that my brain balked as it kicked into translation mode, hoping against hope that he hadn't really just asked me if I had a recipe for tortoise soup. Directing the torch beam towards Guzim's hand I shuddered in disgust when I saw that the object he was holding aloft was indeed a sizeable tortoise, its creased head puckering back into its shell as though objecting to the sudden flash of light. My repugnance was not directed at the noble creature but at the prospect of Guzim turning this member of a protected species into soup.

I must confess to a certain fondness for tortoises that stretches back to my schooldays when Derek Little became the first of my classmates to acquire one as a pet, showing off his exotic prize by smuggling it into the classroom in his satchel. It struck me as unbearably cruel to confine the prehistoric looking animal to the Little's living room, leaving it to sluggishly roam around on patterned Axmimster instead of grass. Here in Greece I had been delighted to discover wild tortoises roaming freely and regarded with great respect by the locals. It wasn't uncommon to witness cars swerving to avoid a tortoise slowly crossing the road, the driver often pulling over to pick up the creature and deposit it safely in an olive grove, offering protection from oncoming traffic. Speeding motorists might think nothing of leaving splattered foxes and cats in their wake on the mountain road, but their attitude to preserving the tortoise population was one I found most commendable.

Although I had no idea if tortoise meat was a regular item on Albanian menus, I was familiar with the popularity of turtles as an English delicacy during the eighteenth and nineteenth centuries. Turtle soup was at one time all the rage at dinner parties for the landed gentry, but the exorbitant cost of importing turtles from the West Indies led to its decline and its replacement with mock turtle soup. My well-thumbed copy of Mrs Beeton features just such a recipe, but since it involves boiling half a calf's head I haven't been tempted to experiment.

As Guzim's words raced through my mind visions of Derek Little's bulging school satchel vied with images of vast tureens of mock turtle soup. Recalling that the Greek language does not have separate words for turtle and tortoise, *helona* covering both, I considered perhaps Guzim had happened across some age-old recipe for turtle soup and mixed up his breeds. The thought of him butchering the innocent tortoise to satisfy his selfish greed warranted the sternest admonishment. Drawing myself up to my full height I directed a scathing look at Guzim, though admittedly it was so dark it was probably a pointless gesture.

BUCKET TO GREECE (VOL. 6)

"*Tha prepei na drepeste, einai varvari na trote chelones.*"

"What was that Victor, I didn't quite get it?" Barry hissed.

"I said he should be ashamed of himself, it is barbaric to eat tortoises."

"He wants to eat that tortoise…"

Barry's words were cut off midsentence by Guzim loudly proclaiming, "*Oti itan ena asteio,*" it was a joke. Since I failed to laugh Guzim insisted he wouldn't eat it: "*Den tha to fame.*"

Guzim began to rattle off some feeble sounding excuse which began to sound less pathetic by the moment. As he told us that he had been lurking by the vegetable patch in an attempt to discover the mysterious culprit that had been munching its way through the lettuces, I recalled that the salad greens had indeed been displaying marked evidence of bite marks of late. Guzim assured us that now he had identified the guilty party he could protect the lettuce crop by isolating the tortoise in the chicken run where it could nibble away at the straggly dandelions to its heart's content without destroying my salad ingredients.

Finally satisfied that Guzim had no intention of cooking up the tortoise I agreed to his suggestion of housing it with the chickens. There was plenty of space in the chicken run for the tortoise to wander at leisure and the netting would provide a secure barrier if Cynthia's foul cat came calling; her vile mutant would attempt to mate with anything. With the matter settled Guzim adjourned to his shed for the night, cackling with laughter as he repeated the preposterous suggestion "*soupa helona.*"

With the coast finally clear I reminded Barry we needed to get a move on shifting the bathtub. "Guzim's antics have delayed us and you don't want to get a dressing down from Anne Trout."

"She can whistle if she thinks I'd answer to her," Barry said defiantly as we entered the downstairs storage room. "Ooh, it's lovely and cool in here, I'm almost tempted to just sleep here in the tub and drag it out tomorrow, but Cynthia will likely need a hand with the baby. Put your back into it Victor, this thing weighs a ton."

Pushing and pulling the cast iron tub we finally manoeuvred it into position, well away from prying eyes behind the new grape arbor. Bidding goodnight to Barry I wandered over to the chicken run. I was pleased to see that the tortoise appeared to have settled comfortably into its new habitat and I hoped that the chickens would make if feel welcome. Smiling contentedly I made my way back to the house, eager to tell Marigold about the latest addition to the Bucket household.

Chapter 9

A Rather Disturbing Call

Marigold had already retired to bed by the time I made it indoors, her nose stuck in one of her moving abroad books. It seemed that our own adventurous move had done nothing to dampen her insatiable appetite for the genre.

"Turn the air-con up a notch Victor, and don't forget to put another tablet in the anti-mosquito plug in," she instructed, her eyes glued to the page.

As I busied myself preparing for bed I filled

her in on the latest addition to the Bucket household, mulling Marigold's advice that I would need to keep an eye on the chickens to ensure they didn't start pecking at the tortoise until we could ascertain if they were compatible. "We must come up with a name for it. Is it a girl or a boy?"

"I've no idea, it was very dark outside," I hedged, having no clue how one went about determining the sex of a tortoise. "I'd hazard a guess by its size that it's pretty ancient, tortoises are renowned for their longevity. I suppose as we named all the chickens after Greek drinks, we could continue the tradition."

"I think there's only *Frappé* left that we haven't used, after that we will simply have to resort to calling them English drinks with a Greek accent, like *votka* and *sampania*."

"*Frappé* it is then…who on earth could be calling at this late hour? I hope that Geraldine hasn't been ghosted already, if she's calling to cry on your shoulder I will tell her to call back tomorrow, it's much too late in the day for you to endure her histrionics now," I said churlishly, heading into the grand salon to answer the telephone.

"Vic, is that you Vic?" a male voice I didn't

recognise badgered excitedly when I answered the phone.

"Victor," I corrected, having a loathing for the shortened version of my name.

"It's me Duggie." I was none the wiser and struggled to put a face to the name. "Duggie, you remember, we exchanged numbers when we met at the funeral."

"Ah, Douglas...I must say it's something of a shock to hear from you," I stuttered, sinking onto the sofa in bewilderment. Clawsome immediately threw herself onto my lap, curling up into a ball. Grateful for her comforting presence I stroked the cat unthinkingly, my mind occupied with memories of my trip back to England the previous summer with Violet Burke.

My mother didn't go into too much detail about how she had finally managed to track down Vic, the ever elusive sweet-talking soap salesman who she was pretty certain, after a process of elimination, had fathered me. Vic had seduced Violet Bloom during the war, plying her with hard to get soap, but did a runner before she had time to break the news that he had knocked her up. Violet surmised that Vic had not necessarily run away from her, but rather fled the military police that were in hot pursuit of him for going AWOL. She confided that she never really bought his tall tale that he had been medically discharged from the army; his fake injury wasn't at all convincing, his habit of limping on alternate legs being a bit of a giveaway.

Violet Bloom never heard from Vic again after he had done a runner, an ironic action to take considering his supposed shrapnel injury. All her efforts to locate him as her stomach expanded proved fruitless. His cowardly midnight flit left her with nothing more than bitter memories of laundry soap as she recalled how he would always scour his hands in cheap suds after a tumble. Alone and jilted, facing the stigma of being a single mother, Violet Burke was forced into the agonising decision to abandon me in a bucket at the railway station. It was only when the two of us were reunited and I expressed an interest in learning more about my father, that Violet Burke made a concerted effort to track down the absconded travelling salesman.

Just before my mother arrived in Meli the previous summer she had managed to pin Vic down to an address in Macclesfield. We flew back to England together, our trip to Macclesfield delayed until my mother could rearrange her shifts in the chippy. The two day delay didn't make any difference as it turned out because Vic had already kicked the bucket before we'd even stepped on the plane to England; however the delay did mean that our arrival in Macclesfield coincided with the departure of the funeral cortege from the terraced house where Vic had gasped his last breath.

"Looks like someone round here is set to be buried," my mother said, observing the hearse parked in the street as she knocked on the door of the address she had tracked him down to.

After an interminable wait the door was thrust open by a large formidable looking woman in her seventies, battle grey hair and a dowdy black suit that had seen better days accentuating the overall image of frumpiness. I couldn't help notice that with her rather busty and bulbous figure she projected a marked resemblance to my mother, though she obviously made less effort with her appearance, neglecting to experiment with the hair dye. Sharp eyes that gave the impression of never missing a trick peered out from her makeup free face; looking us up and down suspiciously she dispensed with the civilities, abruptly demanding to know what we wanted.

BUCKET TO GREECE (VOL. 6)

"We're after Vic, we have it on good authority he lives at this address," my mother said standing her ground firmly.

"You debt collectors don't half pick your moment to come calling, just tacky it is. Well you're out of luck, you can whistle if you think I'm settling his debts," the woman retorted in a manner that struck me as a tad vulgar, moving to slam the door in our faces, only thwarted by the timely imposition of Vi's foot.

"Do we look like debt collectors?" my mother snapped, her words echoing my own thoughts; I found it quite ludicrous that anyone could confuse me with the sort of heavy who went round threatening to break legs. "We're not here for money, we're looking for Vic."

"Whatever you want with Vic, you're too late, he'll be six foot under within the hour," the woman barked, waving towards the hearse. Although I felt a sinking feeling, Violet Burke wasn't having any of it, convinced it was a clever ruse to get rid of us.

"A likely tale, very convenient I must say for the old bugger to go and snuff it just to avoid facing up to his fatherly responsibilities at last," my mother said, scepticism plastered all over her features. "Look there's no point you making excuses for him; we're not budging till we've confronted him. Just tell Vic we're here, it's beyond time that he met his son and namesake."

"I'm not spinning a yarn, he really is dead. He keeled over last week. His son you say...you do have a look of our Terrance about you," the woman said, giving me the once over before turning to Vi. "What did you say your name was?"

"I didn't, but it's Violet Burke, Blossom what was back when I knew Vic..."

"Aye, I've heard him mention you once or twice; he liked to hark back to the past when he had a drink inside him. I suppose you'd better come in, we don't want to be washing our dirty laundry in front of the whole street, nowt the nosy buggers round here like more than a bit of juicy gossip," she grumbled.

As we stepped inside the woman bellowed "Terry, get yourself in here," before giving my mother the once over. "Violet Blossom, fancy you turning up here. I suppose he's been carrying on with you behind my back, he never could keep it in his trousers."

"I haven't seen him since the war," my mother stated flatly. "I take it you're Vic's wife then?"

BUCKET TO GREECE (VOL. 6)

"Common law wife is all; I never could pin Vic down with the legalities. I'm Barb by the way, Barb Foot," she said before once again yelling for Terry.

"Keep your hair on Mum, there's another ten minutes before we have to bury him," a male voice bellowed back.

Turning the full force of her attention on me Barb repeated "You really do have a look of our Terrance about you, no doubt of that."

"Terrance?" I questioned.

"My lad. What did you say your name was?"

"Victor."

"Vic never mentioned a Victor...the cheating love rat usually owned up to his offspring if any slappers turned up after child support; mind you he did always try to wriggle his way out of paying it."

"I'm hardly a child in need of supporting," I pointed out, beginning to get the impression that Vic had perhaps spawned more than one Bucket.

"So I suppose you've rolled up hoping for a hand out from his inheritance. Well there isn't any money to be had, so you've had a wasted trip," Barb said.

"How were we supposed to know he's dead? It's sixty years since I saw hide or hair of him…" Violet Burke protested.

"So you haven't been doing the dirty with Vic behind my back?" Barb raised her eyebrows questioningly.

"For goodness sake, I told you I haven't clapped eyes on him since the war. Victor here was curious about his father, that's the only reason we're here," my mother insisted. "I've got more self-respect than to carry on with an army deserter that deserted me in my hour of need."

There was barely room to stand in the small living room that Barb Foot ushered us into, the floor space dominated by two huge black leather sofas. The seats, encased in protective clear plastic, bore visible signs of posterior imprints, so I presumed the plastic was strategically placed to prevent the leather from becoming tarnished. Barb obviously took pride in keeping a neat home; the room was conspicuously clean, the whiff of bleach emanating from the brilliant white net curtains clashing with the overpowering smell of furniture polish. A set of pristine encyclopaedias that didn't look as though they'd ever be opened visibly weighed down the sagging shelf giving them house room.

BUCKET TO GREECE (VOL. 6)

My eyes were inexorably drawn to a framed photograph of a man that took pride of place on the mantelpiece. Moving towards it, curious if I was about to see an image of Vic for the first time, I was distracted by the entrance of a tall man in a black suit, his head down as he struggled to knot his tie. "Here give me a hand with this Mum, the last time I was forced to wear one of these was when I was up before the beak."

As he straightened up I got my first full look at him; it was a physical jolt to my senses. It was like looking in a mirror.

"This is our Terrance," Barb said, emitting a low whistle as her head swivelled between the two of us. "Like peas in a pod, no question. Terry, it looks like another half-brother of yours has turned up out of the woodwork."

Staring at this stranger sibling I realised my initial impression of an obvious likeness between us was perhaps a tad hasty. Although we were much of an age Terrance's lank and straggly hair was clearly in dire need of a good cut, and was peppered with grey, whereas my own grey had been concealed with a subtle application of the Grecian 2000 left behind in Harold's bathroom cabinet. The jacket of his suit strained to contain his stomach and his chin was a tad jowly, whereas regular walks in the countryside and a healthy Greek diet have helped to maintain my trim figure. Terrance's complexion had the ruddy look of a seasoned drinker, whereas I only drink in moderation and carefully protect my skin with regular applications of a high factor sun screen.

Terrance momentarily blanched as he took in my appearance. Lighting a cigarette he recovered his composure, saying "That's handy you turning up now, you can chip in with the funeral expenses, it's a right rip-off. I was all for putting him in a cardboard box but Mum wouldn't have it."

"The only reason we are here today is so I could make Vic's acquaintance and ascertain if he was indeed my absconded parent," I said firmly.

"I don't think there's any doubt that you're Vic's lad, you and Terrance are the spit of one another," Barb said.

"You can't go getting off scot-free, if he was your father you have an obligation to chip in towards the coffin, fair's fair, split it four ways between us brothers," Terrance said.

"Let it go Terry, he's just said he never even met your dad. I think Vic likely didn't know of this one's existence, he would have had something to say if he did," Barb said sagely before walking over to the mantelpiece to retrieve the framed photograph. Without saying a word she passed it to Violet Burke who said "That's Vic and no mistake."

"Aye well he aged a bit after that was taken; it must have been what, 1968, just before he pulled one of his regular disappearing acts," Barb said. My mother passed the photograph to me. Looking at the image of my father I didn't feel any particular sense of connection and I bore less of a resemblance to him than I did to my newly discovered half-brother. The photograph of Vic captured the image of a cocky looking chap oozing confidence; he was clearly a bit of a spiv.

"Yes, it was definitely '68, I remember 'cos our Terrance had just turned eighteen. It was another year and a half before he turned up again like the proverbial bad penny…"

I was taken aback as I absorbed this information, calculating that Terrance was six years my junior even though I had initially assumed there wasn't much difference in our ages.

"'68 was when he started that spell in Strangeways, Mum," Terrance interrupted.

Loud banging on the door interspersed with shouts of "Come on Barb, let's get this show on the road," allowed no time for me to process the notion that my absconded father had been a villainous jailbird.

"I suppose it would be only fitting if the pair of you came along to the funeral," Barb said. Keen to glean more information I looked at my mother; she nodded her acquiescence.

Being unfamiliar with the area we agreed to leave the hire car behind and piled into the lead funeral car with Barb and Terrance, where we were joined by a rather short and jovial looking fellow. I received yet another shock to the system when Terrance introduced him as my half-brother, Douglas. Barb was quick to point out that Douglas was the off-spring of some other slapper Vic had taken up with during one of his disappearances.

"Vic, are you there Vic? These long distance phone lines can be a bit temperamental. It's me Duggie, your brother." His voice roused me from my reverie.

"Half-brother," I automatically corrected. "Yes, I'm here Douglas; it's just something of a surprise to hear from you." Even though I vaguely recalled exchanging numbers with Douglas at the wake, I hadn't expected to ever hear from him again.

"I wanted to let you know that me, the missus and the kiddies will be over your way next week, we got a last minute package and fly out on Sunday. Can't wait to see you again, we've got fifty years of catching up to do."

Chapter 10

Loosely Related Strangers

"Victor, you look as though you have seen a ghost, Victor," Marigold said, a touch of alarm in her voice, peering at me through sleepy eyes when I returned to the bedroom.

"Your ghostly reference is quite apt. It looks as though I am about to be haunted by a part of my past that I had no idea existed until that trip back to England with Vi last summer," I said.

"Must you talk in riddles? I take it that was your mother on the phone. Is she planning another visit? I hope you didn't complain too much about her reversing the charges again, you know how difficult it is for her to manage on what she earns in the chippy."

"It wasn't my mother as it happens, it was one of my newly discovered half-brothers," I said, giving Marigold a moment to let this unexpected information sink in.

"Oh gosh, which one?" All trace of sleep was gone from her voice as she prepared to grill me.

"Douglas."

"Was he the one that made a scene at the wake, demanding you contribute to the funeral costs?"

"No, that was Terrance..."

"Ah, your doppelganger," Marigold said, attempting to stifle a snort of amusement.

"Only at first glance, I don't think there is any chance anyone would actually mistake me for Terrance..."

"I'm only going off what Vi had to say, she insisted he was the spit of you..."

"Maybe if I'd let myself go and didn't bother to take any pride in my appearance," I replied peevishly. Undoubtedly there were obvious similarities in our appearance, but I preferred not to draw parallels since our characters were starkly dissimilar. Terrance struck me as a bit of a chancer, a trait likely exacerbated by living with our reprobate father, whilst the scene he had made at the wake led me to believe he had inherited his mother's rather vulgar streak.

"I'm still curious to see for myself," Marigold said. "You can't blame me. I married an abandoned orphan and now it turns out you have three half-siblings. Naturally my interest is piqued." After meeting two of my half-brothers at my father's funeral I wasn't particularly keen to make the acquaintance of the third one who hadn't bothered showing up for the burial.

"Well it looks as though you are about to have the chance to meet Douglas. He's flying into Greece with his family this Sunday and wants us all to get together. I'm afraid he rather steamrolled me into it."

"I can't possibly have the place ready for houseguests by Sunday, it's awfully short notice and the place is an absolute tip," Marigold proclaimed. Admittedly she had taken a rather lackadaisical approach to sweeping and mopping in the last couple of days, but I recognised this as a cunning ploy to wear me down into purchasing the coveted Roomba.

"There's no need to prepare for house-guests," I hastily reassured my wife. "They are coming in on a package and staying down on the coast. I jotted down the name of the accommodation and agreed we would meet them there on Monday evening."

Marigold exhaled in obvious relief that the Bucket household wasn't about to be overrun with loosely related strangers. Relieved that their holiday accommodation was all arranged at a suitable distance my wife warmed up to the idea of a brotherly reunion, reminding me that I hadn't found anything objectionable about Douglas.

"We only met briefly but he did seem quite harmless," I acknowledged, recalling that Douglas had accepted the unexpected announcement that he had another half-brother with remarkable equanimity. Although I had been too shell shocked by the day's events to make much of an effort to acquaint myself with the details of Douglas' life, he had seemed keen to foster a relationship, whilst Terrance's uncouth behaviour had made me equally keen to flee the scene.

When the funeral cortege had pulled up at

the church I held back, not keen on the idea of mingling with the mourners or of explaining my non-existent relationship to the newly deceased. Terrance and Douglas stepped forward to serve as pall bearers, whilst Barb Foot made her way into the church. Callous though it may sound, I didn't feel particularly inclined to attend the service; it seemed hypocritical to pretend to mourn the man I had never met who had abandoned the mother I was growing increasingly fond of. I hadn't had time to fully process the events of the day; expecting to at long last come face-to-face with my father, it was rather a shock to the system to learn my timing was off.

"Do you want to go inside for the service?" I asked my mother solicitously, concerned how she was taking the sudden news that Vic had croaked it. It may well be sixty years since she'd seen him, but obviously they had shared an intimate closeness, or I wouldn't be here.

"I'd rather wait out here and just make sure he's buried," Violet Burke admitted, still appearing rather sceptical that Vic was actually dead.

"Oi Vic, get over here and give us a shoulder, we're a man down 'cos our Jimmy hasn't turned up," Terrance yelled over from the church porch, violating the quiet solemnity of the occasion. As I hesitated, reluctant to insert myself into the proceedings, Terrance reiterated his demand. "The least you can do is help to carry the old git inside seeing that you don't want to cough up towards his coffin."

Smarting with embarrassment at being singled out in front of the mourners I reluctantly stepped forward, taking the weight of the coffin on one shoulder. Wearing tan slacks and a blue blazer I felt inappropriately attired for the occasion amidst the sea of black. Looking across at my mother I watched as she tied a transparent rain bonnet in place, no doubt covering her hair as a mark of respect. I was sure that Violet Burke must be kicking herself; if she had known we were rocking up to Vic's funeral she would have splashed out on a suitable hat. My mother has a real weakness for hats.

Feeling uncomfortable standing in for the missing Jimmy, whoever he was, I was relieved that the service was mercifully short and devoid of any personal eulogies. A couple of the members of the congregation made no attempt to hide their snorts of derision when the vicar threw in some vacuous generalities attempting to paint the deceased in a good light, prompting

V.D. BUCKET

the vicar to become so flustered he wound things up rather prematurely.

Roped in to help carry the coffin out to the newly dug grave I steeled myself against the cold drizzle, feeling detached from the proceedings. I was left unmoved by Barb Foot's brazen scene of hollow grief by the graveside, wailing piteously as the black veil trimming her hat clung damply to her face like a bedraggled fishing net. No sooner had the first clod of earth landed on the sunken coffin than Barb Foot made a remarkable recovery, practically sprinting to the funeral car.

"Oi Vic, get a move on, you're wasting valuable drinking time. We're off to the pub to raise a glass to Dad, come on," Terrance bellowed.

"We've got no choice," Violet Burke hissed. "You left the hire car back at their place."

Even though I live in a foreign country I have never felt more out of place than I did at Vic's wake. I found the boozy send-off arranged for the father I had never met a cringe fest of embarrassment. The moment we entered the dreary public house Terrance ordered drinks all round, proposing a toast to his departed father. In no time at all Barb Foot became vocally maudlin, unable to hold her port and lemon. Sidling over to Violet Burke she raised a glass to her common-law husband, before wasting no time in slagging him off.

"I don't know how I put up with Vic and his philandering ways. He was a smarmy git and no mistake."

"I take it he still had the gift of the gab then," my mother said.

"Aye, he could always talk me into taking him back after he'd pulled one of his disappearing acts. Lucky for him the women he took up with didn't catch up with him again until after he'd got his feet well and truly back under my table. He was always careful not to do the dirty on his own doorstep; his job as a travelling salesman gave him plenty of opportunity to keep his cheating ways under wraps," Barb said.

"Still selling soap was he?"

"He'd flog anything that would bring in a few bob, from encyclopaedias to vacuum cleaners," Barb said, her words explaining the out of place untouched tomes of knowledge in her living room. "He had all those bored housewives eating out of the palm of his hand. Course that fraud caper he got into was his undoing, but that prison stretch did turn him straight…"

V.D. BUCKET

"It is always reassuring to hear that prison can effectively serve to rehabilitate," I chimed in.

"Well I wouldn't say Vic was rehabilitated as such but he hated Strangeways with a vengeance, it was that filthy in there that he vowed he'd never go back. It was the fungus in the showers he couldn't bear; he was paranoid about picking up a nasty foot infection, he reckoned the showers were swimming in warts and athlete's foot, bleedin' breeding grounds for festering germs he used to swear."

I shuddered in sympathy. From what my mother had told me Vic was a tad germaphobic; squalid and unsanitary prison conditions must have been sheer torture for a man with an obsessive compulsion for scouring his hands.

"So you took him back after prison?" my mother asked Barb.

"Well I was going to until that slapper turned up with a visiting pass. I see she didn't bother showing up today..."

"Who's that Mum?" Terrance slurred, exhaling beery fumes as he practically fell into the seat next to his mother.

"Joyce."

"Jimmy's not here neither," Terrance said.

BUCKET TO GREECE (VOL. 6)

Seeing the baffled look on my face Terrance dropped the bombshell, "Jimmy's your other brother, a right stuck up tosser, ain't he Mum."

"Well he got that off Joyce, she always did give herself airs and graces even though she was all fur coats and no knickers."

"This is all rather a lot to take in," I admitted, trying to get to grips with the surprise news that in the space of one morning I had acquired three half-brothers.

"I'll give you the potted version shall I?" Terrance offered. "Mum took Dad back after he did the dirty on her with Duggie's mum Sharon, but she warned him it would be the last time. Then dad did another of his disappearing tricks back in '68 and we didn't hear nothing about him for eighteen months when we found out he was doing time. Mum being soft like, started visiting, three buses it took her, but then she found out he'd been prison two-timing her when that slapper Joyce turned up at Strangeways with Jimmy in tow…"

"Jimmy was the spit of our Terrance when he was a toddler…" Barb interrupted.

"Turned out he'd been living with Joyce when he got arrested and Jimmy was his going away present," Terrance said.

"And Vic never breathed a word he'd had another nipper. I told him we were finished, but he came crawling back when he got released..."

"You were always a soft touch, letting him smarm his way back in with fancy soap and a bottle of port," Terrance interrupted. "That Joyce wouldn't have him back when she found out about you Mum, he'd made out he was footloose and fancy free."

"And I was the mug that took him back. But to be fair until Victor here turned up today I never heard of Vic fathering another sprog after Jimmy..."

Attempting to come to terms with this overload of information I excused myself and stepped into the car park, relieved to escape the smoky confines of the seedy pub. I shivered in the light drizzle; this was not the July weather I was slowly adapting to in Greece. Drawing a mental picture of my new family tree I gasped as I realised that my youngest half-brother Jimmy must be the same age as Benjamin and I pondered what reason he had for not turning up for his father's burial. My other new half-brother Douglas joined me in the car park but I was a tad too distracted to take in much of what he had to say.

BUCKET TO GREECE (VOL. 6)

When the drizzle turned into a downpour we returned to the pub where the barman phoned for a taxi to take us back to the car. Our return indoors prompted the by-now well lubricated Terrance to make a scene, demanding I cough up towards the funeral expenses. Terrance took a thug-like position, perhaps underestimating me as a bit of a sap. Even though he was egged on by his cronies I stood my ground, proving I was no pushover by resolutely refusing to part with the cash. Douglas took my side, pointing out to our half-brother that I had never even met our mutual father and that Terrance's bullying demands were nothing short of extortion. In an attempt to ward off any fisticuffs I instructed the landlord to charge a round to my credit card; the prospect of free alcohol appeared to somewhat alleviate the tension.

I was desperately relieved when the call 'Taxi for Bucket' offered an escape route; the funeral wake appeared to be in danger of descending into an undignified drunken fracas.

"I feel sorry for you Victor, being related to that lot, they weren't half common," my mother said as the taxi pulled away. "You know, it's a good job I gave you up, if Vic had stuck around and we'd raised you together you might have turned out like that miserable lot instead of nice and respectable."

The phone call from Douglas was the first I'd heard from any member of my newly discovered family since the funeral fiasco and the thought of meeting up with him left me a tad uneasy. As an abandoned orphan I had not yet grown accustomed to the idea of siblings.

"Don't be such a worrywart Victor, you may enjoy meeting Douglas. After all, look how your mother has grown on you," Marigold taunted me as she turned off the bedside lamp.

Chapter 11

A Brief Brush with the Law

"I do appreciate you giving me a lift to the office Victor," Cynthia said as she joined me in the Punto after stashing a few bulky carrier bags in my boot. I couldn't fail to notice her eyes were visibly puffy, a condition she explained away by telling me she'd been bawling since dawn at the prospect of being parted from Anastasia for the first time.

"But surely she is in good hands with your parents," I said cautiously in light of Barry's misgivings about his in-laws.

V.D. BUCKET

"Mother hasn't been very hands on so far, she's very good at barking instructions...but as she keeps reminding me it is her first ever foreign holiday and she wants to make the most of it and get a tan," Cynthia spluttered before breaking down in tears. "I do hope that Marigold pops over today, she's such a natural with the baby and I've a terrible feeling that my mother rather views Anastasia as a nuisance."

Barry and I had pleaded with Marigold to keep her distance today and let Anne Trout get on with it without her assistance. The sooner the Trout woman was exposed to the actual nitty-gritty of caring for her granddaughter, the sooner she was likely to pack her bags and leave Meli, particularly since Cynthia wouldn't be around to wait on her hand and foot. Although neither Barry nor I was convinced that Marigold would take a blind bit of notice of our request, I was confident that her hands would be so full preparing for the ex-pat dinner party that she may not have time to visit; after all it takes Marigold an absolute age to scale and gut a fish and she would need to confront more than one for a giant pan of fish soup.

"So how is my adorable niece this morning?" I asked.

"Just perfect," Cynthia said, wiping her tears. "My mother complained the frogs kept her awake croaking all night and threatened to poison the pond with bleach to get rid of them."

"That would be an ecological travesty," I proclaimed in disgust.

"That's why I took the precaution of collecting up every bottle of household detergent and putting them in your boot."

"A wise move," I commended, hoping the Trout woman wouldn't manage to identify bleach on the shelves in the village shop; most likely if she felt so inclined the foreign letters would flummox her. "Are you looking forward to returning to work?"

"I am, apart from being separated from the baby. I'm not sure I'm really cut out to be a stay at home mum, I'm not used to having time on my hands; returning to work part-time offers a nice balance. Are you doing the Vathia trip today?"

"I am, it's my favourite excursion even though the journey is such a long one."

In order to meet and greet the day-trippers signed up for today's trip I first had to drive to the office in town. Once everyone was counted off the coach would then depart for our destination, practically retracing the route I would take during my drive to the office. Rinsing and repeating the whole rigmarole later to return the trippers to town made for an exhausting day. Fortunately with Sakis at the wheel of the coach I would be able to relax and enjoy the scenery, when I wasn't delivering my informative spiels.

Cynthia emitted a soft snore. Supposing she must be shattered from broken nights with the baby I didn't take offence at her falling asleep on me before we had barely left the village. Thinking of the long workday ahead I sighed with anticipation at the prospect of sneaking in a luxuriant bubble bath before Marigold's dinner party. I had crept out at first light to admire the well-scrubbed cast iron bath tub in its new discreet setting. Barry had come up trumps, carving a neat shelf into one of the wooden pillars that would support the grapevine and adding a couple of hooks. A bottle of bubble bath waited on the shelf and one of my treasured esoteric back scratchers dangled from a hook. All I needed to do was to hook up a hosepipe to our outside tap. Since the pipe that fed the tap was above ground I always needed to run the water for several minutes to run off the hot to avoid scalding the growing veggies; later I would simply divert the hot water into the tub.

Reaching the flat coastal stretch I noticed a large group of Albanian men hanging around at the bus stop, the preferred pick up point for those seeking manual labourers. With Athens due to host the Olympic Games in August there was a lot of interest focused on Greece and an uptick in English people looking at properties on the coast. This in turn fuelled the rise in immigrant labourers looking for casual work in the building trade, the paltry wages on offer a fortune compared to the pittance they could earn back home.

A couple of shady looking types were openly glugging from beer bottles, reminding me that Guzim's preferred breakfast used to be a bottle of Amstel before he reformed his ways. Recently Guzim had managed to secure more regular gardening work in Meli, alleviating the need for him to moped down to the coast so often, a blessing indeed since he was often forced to push the dated contraption back up the hill after a hard day's work. Giannis the bee man had been mulling the idea of expanding into breeding rabbits for meat, an idea he was able to begin to implement when he discovered Guzim was experienced in cuniculture. Guzim remained ignorant to the meaning of the word cuniculture since it didn't appear to have a Greek translation and I wasn't prepared to venture into tackling the Albanian language. I was glad that Guzim's ability to have his fingers in many pies spared him from the necessity of competing for work with his compatriots at the bus stop; his slight stature invariably meant he was overlooked and the last to be picked, which did nothing to improve his surliness.

Despite the early hour cars were beginning to congregate at the side of the road where narrow tracks led down to hidden coves. I imagined keen swimmers taking to the water before the day really heated up and sun worshippers already sprawled out on the secluded pebble beaches below. Of course the cars may have been left there overnight, their occupants having the romantic notion of sleeping under the stars. I doubted any of them would repeat the adventure if they woke up to discover they had been gullible fodder for numerous sand flies feasting on their flesh. I made a mental note to bring Marigold to one of these delightful spots for a swim; she would appreciate the change of scene from our usual sandy beach.

BUCKET TO GREECE (VOL. 6)

Cynthia stirred beside me as the Punto bounced over a narrow ridge sliced into the tarmac, intended for an electrical wire. As she came out of her stupor panic immediately replaced her languid yawn and she fumbled for her mobile phone, desperate to call home and check up on the baby.

"We've made excellent time so far," I said. "Why don't I park up near the *Dimarcheio* and fetch us a couple of takeaway coffees whilst you make your call.

"That's so thoughtful of you Victor, a coffee is just what I need."

As I waited for the coffees my senses were assaulted with the mouth-watering aroma of freshly baked *krouasan sokolates*, *milopites* and *bougatsas*. Not wishing to litter the Punto with phyllo crumbs from chocolate croissants, apples pies or cream filled pastries, I resisted temptation, reminding myself I had eaten a perfectly adequate breakfast of muesli topped with fresh strawberries from the garden. A sudden image of Terrance's gut straining against his shirt offered a salutary reminder of the fate awaiting my body if I gave in to greed.

Returning to the car with the coffees I felt a twinge of momentary guilt when Cynthia disclosed she hadn't had time to grab any breakfast because she'd had her hands full with the baby. I reminded her that we'd be in town in fifty minutes and she could buy something from the café across the road from the office. Cynthia told me that her mother had complained that an overweight Greek woman who couldn't speak a word of English was currently sitting in the kitchen making a fuss of the baby and Mrs Trout didn't know how to get rid of her. "I wonder who it can be," Cynthia said.

"Perhaps it is Kyria Kompogiannopoulou," I suggested.

"Oh I do hope so; she has such a way with babies." Cynthia perked up at the thought of the doting Greek *yiayia* overseeing her mother's care of the baby. "You should have seen the darling pink bonnet and matching booties she knitted for the baby, though I must confess I do worry about Anastasia overheating in all that wool."

"It seems the Greek grannies have a mortal fear of babies being exposed to the slightest draught."

"Can you imagine how many layers they'll be demanding I wrap Anastasia up in once winter comes," Cynthia giggled. "I was finding their fussing a bit much at first but then I realised how genuine their affection is... I really shouldn't say this but it makes me notice the difference between their hands-on approach and mother's rather standoffish ways. She seems to selfishly think Anastasia's needs should come second to her own demands."

"Well you'll get a break this evening. Marigold has invited your parents to attend the monthly meeting of the ex-pat dining club," I said.

"Oh I know, it was such a relief when Barry told me, it means I don't need to cook for them."

"Surely your parents muck in with the cooking?"

"Mother says she can't be expected to know what to do with Greek ingredients in a confusing foreign kitchen," Cynthia sighed. "To be fair the bus and train journey across Europe rather took it out of her and she needs to catch up on her rest."

"You should introduce her to the English supplies Harold left behind in the kitchen; surely your mother must be capable of throwing a Fray Bentos pie in the oven or opening a can of beans," I suggested, feeling suitably appalled that Anne Trout was deliberately creating extra work for the new mother. It was Cynthia who should be taking it easy, not the spoiled selfish snob who had meandered to Greece at a leisurely pace, being pampered in plush hotels along the way.

"That's an idea. Although mother likes to pretend that she wouldn't give houseroom to a Fray Bentos I know she always kept a secret stash at home," Cynthia said. "Quite why she maintains an aubergine is too much of a foreign culinary challenge is beyond me, she must have seen them in Waitrose."

"Let me know if you need any, I've a bumper crop this year…"

"That's so kind of you, with all the renovation work I haven't had chance to get started establishing a vegetable patch yet."

"Let's just hope your mother doesn't develop pretentions for eating frogs' legs otherwise she may cook up the contents of your pond."

"No chance of that, she isn't impressed with French food."

"That's a shame since Marigold is rustling up a French bouillabaisse this evening. I'll give her the heads up so that she can pass it off as an Italian cioppino," I said, relieved that there would be no Greek guests attending who would realise my authentic recipe for *psarosoupa* was being culturally appropriated.

We fell into an easy silence as the journey progressed, Cynthia seemingly captivated by the spectacular views. The sun reflected the sea off to one side of the road, beyond the sheer drop, and the trees stood to attention in the olive groves, not the slightest breeze ruffling their silvery leaves. The villages we drove through bustled with life, elderly gents claiming their regular seats outside cafés where they would nurse miniature cups of Greek coffee while watching the world go by, shopkeepers hosing water over their outdoor displays of fresh vegetables. The Punto was submerged in shadow as we drove through the gorge and navigated the twist of the ancient bridge, before following the road ever upwards towards the summit.

By the time the town appeared on the horizon Cynthia was dozing again and I found myself singing along with Sakis Rouvas as the familiar refrain of 'Shake It' came over the radio. Vangelis and Athena had dragged Marigold and I along to watch the televised Eurovision Song Contest in a coastal taverna, elated when this year's Greek entry placed third. It never ceases to surprise me how popular this puerile annual event is in our adopted homeland; in comparison it was primarily treated with derision back in England. Whilst I personally considered this year's tune a tad irritating, there was no doubt it was catchy enough to get under my skin. The shaking Sakis bore quite a strong resemblance to Giannis the bee man, though Giannis, preferring the natural look, did not emulate the handsome pop star's greasy habit of oiling his hair.

Cynthia woke up again as the Punto tackled the hair-pin bends on the downward approach to town. "We should make this a regular thing Victor; it's been quite blissful being able to nap. I feel so much more refreshed."

"Happy to have been of service," I said, genuinely pleased to have lightened the load of my sister-in-law by sparing her the drive. "You'll have to coordinate the rota so that we are in town on the same days. I'm up again next Tuesday for the lazy day cruise."

"That reminds me, Captain Vasos sent the most adorable baby gift, a blue and white sailor outfit with a matching hat; such a thoughtful gesture. It does make Anastasia look like a very cute boy, but she's too young to know the difference." Cynthia's words made me chuckle; it struck me as so unlikely for the half-cut *Kapetanios*, who spent half his life in a manky tee-shirt stiff with old sweat, to choose baby clothes. It would have been more in character for him to send something alcoholic to wet the baby's head.

"I'd better try and make myself look presentable before we reach the office," Cynthia said, attempting to apply her lipstick by contorting in front of the wing mirror as we reached town and took the seafront road. I made a mental note to avoid the seafront on the way back later as it would be packed with waiters taking their lives in their hands, crossing the busy road to serve drinks on the beach. The practice invariably slowed the traffic to a crawl unless one wanted to take the risk of splattering the seasonal servers.

"You look fine and at least you don't have to wear one of these infernal whistles in the office," I assured her before groaning aloud at the sight of a uniformed police officer indicating I should pull into the lay-by next to his patrol car. Even though I am scrupulously law abiding, I always manage to feel somewhat guilty if pulled over by the police. In this instance I felt particularly apprehensive due to the recent discovery that I was spawned by a fraudster who had served time in prison. Hoping I hadn't unwittingly committed some heinous traffic violation I slowed down and pulled into the lay-by, recalling Spiros' sage advice that if I was ever stopped by the police I should simply present myself as an imbecilic Englishman and parrot the stock phrase *"den katalavaino"* meaning 'I don't understand.' Since this was my first time being stopped by the Greek police I was yet to put his advice to the test.

Winding my window down to the max I noticed my empty coffee cup prominently propped up in the cup holder. Cold sweat erupted in my armpits as I pondered the possibility that I had unwittingly broken the law by drinking coffee whilst driving. Recalling that every Greek I knew drove along with a coffee in one hand and a cigarette in the other, I pulled myself together, hoping to present myself as a poised and upstanding Greek resident.

"*Kalimera*," I greeted the officer with a nervous smile, unable to gauge his expression behind his dark sunglasses.

"*Diavatirio kai asfaleia aftokinitou*," the policeman responded curtly, dispensing with the usual civilities as he requested my passport and car insurance. Fumbling for my wallet to retrieve said documents it struck me that were I to follow Spiros' advice by claiming I didn't understand, I would need to pretend I didn't actually have a clue which documents the policeman required. It seemed simpler all round to meekly comply with the officer's instructions and hand over my passport and insurance. As my documentation was wordlessly scrutinised I took a deep breath, realising the policeman had no way of knowing I was loosely related to a criminal dynasty: at least I presumed my half-brother Terrance had followed in our mutual father's miscreant footsteps since I recalled him making a reference to his being up before the beak. I made a mental note to grill Douglas regarding my new family's possibly extensive criminal history when we got together on Monday. Perhaps his arrival in Greece was a good thing because I still had many unanswered questions pertaining to my father's side of the family.

"*Entaxei,*" the officer said, returning my documents and indicating I could drive on.

"*Entaxei,*" I said, repeating his assertion that everything was okay.

"You handled that so well Victor, I was a gibbering wreck the first time that I was pulled over in Greece," Cynthia said, her voice filled with admiration. "I remember that it was not long after I'd first met Spiros and he'd told me the best thing to do if it happened was to claim I didn't speak Greek and mindlessly repeat *'den katalavaino.'* So when I did get pulled over not long after that conversation I followed Spiros' advice. It was such a stupid thing to do because I understood he wanted my passport, but I just sat their foolishly repeating the same phrase over and over. In the end the policeman had to radio through to ask if anyone back at the station knew the English word for *'diavatirio'* and *'asfaleia.'* I felt like such a silly fraud, not to mention a time waster."

Cynthia's words reassured me that she had been clueless I had actually been anything less than poised. If I had come across to my sister-in-law as calm and collected then no doubt the officer of the law would have gained the same impression. I made a mental note to stop drawing dubious parallels between myself and the suspect stock I came from. After all, as my mother had so astutely pointed out, I am nice and respectable.

Chapter 12

Tickled Pink

My brief brush with the law resulted in my tardy arrival at the tourist office. Day trippers impatiently checked their watches as they queued in an orderly line, eager to claim prime seats on the coach. I made an educated guess that the day's tourists were British, the queue being a bit of a giveaway. Back in May I had led an organised group of Italians and the scrum for the coach had been an unruly free-for all, most undignified. A coachload of Brits certainly made my duties less onerous since there was no language barrier to overcome.

After collecting the list of names from the office I greeted the day trippers, apologising for my tardiness with a light-hearted quip about my recent encounter with the Greek police as I ticked their names off on my clipboard.

"Oh how exciting, is it true that they all carry guns?" a woman in the queue asked, introducing herself as Carole Welford. I duly put a tick by her name and that of her husband Bruce.

"Many of them do," I fudged in response, not entirely sure if all members of the Hellenic police force carried weapons. Although I hadn't noticed if the officer who pulled me over was packing a pistol, I had encountered armed officers when I drove Spiros to the police station in town to retrieve the license plates that had been confiscated when he blatantly parked the hearse under a 'No Parking' sign close to the tax office. It had been rather unnerving to run the gauntlet of police officers holding what appeared, to my untrained eye, to be submachine guns, in order to enter the official building so Spiros could fork over the cash to settle his fine. He maintains to this day that if he'd only had the foresight to check there was a coffin in the back he would have got clean away with parking illegally.

"We saw some Greek motorcycle cops yesterday, so handsome in their uniforms," Carole continued.

"Yes, they do look very smart," I agreed, noting the woman's comments mirrored Marigold's sentiments towards the Greek constabulary. I stifled a smile thinking that my wife would be most impressed when Cynthia regaled her with the tale of my admirable composure during my run in with the law earlier.

I was surprised that only fifteen tourists had signed up for the Vathia trip, a much smaller number than the excursion usually attracted. On the plus side it meant there would be fewer stragglers to round up at each stop, but on the flip side the tips may not amount to much. I was pleased to note that the party included a group of three women, and another pair that weren't obviously coupled. I found that tips from couples could be somewhat stingy as they invariably tipped as one, whilst members of small groups were more inclined to each press an individual gratuity upon me at the end of the trip.

Sakis rolled up armed with frappés for both of us, attempting to be subtle as he cast his eyes over the gathering, no doubt on the lookout for any predatory females he would need to avoid if they fancied their chances chatting up a handsome Greek; there was usually one in any given week with the rather desperate intention of spicing up her vacation with a holiday romance. Fortunately for the state of my marriage they tend to develop crushes on Sakis rather than me, often finding his moustache and Greek accent quite irresistible. When Sakis bemoans "I have the curse of the sex-appeal," I duly sympathise, telling him the same women that find him attractive whilst soaking in the Greek culture probably wouldn't look twice at him back in Manchester. I tell him that he's like ouzo or retsina to the tourist palate; something exotic to sample in Greece, less desirable after a plane ride back to reality. Still, he scorns any advances of tourist flirtation, terrified his girlfriend will get the wrong idea.

The group comprised a mix of middle aged and hale looking elders, all suitably dressed in sturdy shoes and sensible hats. Satisfied that the group didn't appear to feature any ardent groupies desperate to sink their talons into his flesh, Sakis relaxed, slurping his frappé as he settled in behind the wheel. For my part I was very relieved to be spared the addition of any rumbustious little Johnnies amongst the number.

Herding my charges on-board I offered a brief summary of the day's itinerary, explaining we would drive directly to Vathia in the Deep Mani where they would be free to explore the captivating village and roam at leisure amongst the ruins of the fortified tower houses. Afterwards we would head to Gerolimenas for lunch in a port-side taverna where a traditional meal of roast goat, oven baked with artichokes and potatoes in lemon juice and oregano, awaited us. I advised the group that since Sakis may encounter a fair bit of traffic on the road out of town I would hold off on imparting historical details and information until the town was behind us. The handy excuse that I did not want to distract the driver was a convenient ploy to recharge my batteries after the early morning drive; I wanted to enjoy my frappé in peace without being harangued with a volley of inane questions.

As Sakis manoeuvred the coach through town I reflected that the evening ahead certainly offered no prospect of peace since the house would be overrun with ex-pats. As I thought of the meal Marigold planned to serve I hoped that she wouldn't make a total botch of the soup or leave the fish lying around for the cats to get their paws on. In truth I don't trust my wife not to throw a cat mauled fish into the pan if she thinks no one will be any the wiser. Her approach to culinary hygiene can be quite blasé if I am not there to remind her, or nag her as she prefers to label it.

With a house full of guests I would reluctantly be forced to delay my first outdoor bubble bath in Harold's old tub. It was also doubtful that I would have any free time to contact my old friend James, or Scrapes as I more commonly refer to him outside office hours, back in Manchester. Technically speaking James Scraper was one rung above me at the Foods Standard Agency, though his exalted position didn't stand in the way of our friendship.

I had been mulling the notion of reconnecting with Scrapes and floating the idea that I appoint him as the editor of my first completed book. Since I'd had more free time over the winter I had finally managed to finish writing the first draft of my book about up-sticking to Greece. Having reached the end of the book, I discovered, to my complete surprise, that I was still rather in the grip of the writing bug and that I had more of my story to tell. Putting the first manuscript to one side I continued to pen the account of our amusing adventures about moving abroad, fancifully imagining there may well be demand for a sequel.

I have not yet shared the news with my wife that the book is finished, nor have I any intention of allowing her to peruse it until I am confident that every last stray typo has been obliterated. If Marigold gets her hands on it before it has undergone a thorough edit she will badger me relentlessly to litter my prose with superfluous exclamation marks and offer a barrage of unwanted and witless suggestions. As I may have mentioned before I would be as likely to take literary advice from my wife as I would from the cat; her taste in reading matter is often beyond dire.

I had hummed and hawed quite a bit, considering if Scrapes was the man for the job of knocking my manuscript into shape, being realistic enough to realise only a fool thinks he can spot each one of his own blundering errors. Whilst Scrapes undoubtedly has an exacting eye for a stray comma, I still had the odd reservation about releasing my untested manuscript to his critical care. My qualms centred on his failure to appreciate the creative flair I added to my reports on the hygiene atrocities perpetrated by some of the less than salubrious staff in some of Manchester's restaurants and takeaways. Scrapes had the annoying tendency to red-line certain words, adding an explanatory note in the margin claiming the highlighted word sounded pompous or pretentious: perish the thought that my language ever veered towards magniloquence. When penning hygiene reports my choice of words was always carefully measured and in keeping with my judgement that a written account about even the grubbiest kitchen benefits from a turn of phrase imbued with a smatter of sophistication.

However, whilst Scrapes can be a tad hasty to judgemental scorn, he always expressed suitable outrage when sifting through reports from the public that were ridden with misplaced apostrophes or sloppy spelling. The agency encouraged the public to report any instances of poor food safety or hygiene practices in the establishments they frequented. Scrapes was responsible for collating the data and part of my remit involved responding to these reports which we referred to in the business as the

BUCKET TO GREECE (VOL. 6)

Snitches Hotline, even though most reports came in via atrociously written anonymous letters. Often these letters were spiteful ploys by rival businesses to grass up the competition, though naturally the repulsed public did report some of the more disgusting things they chanced to witness. We were often inundated with information about chefs spotted washing their feet in the kitchen sink or waiters picking their noses in full view of the dining room, but these fleeting actions, unless habitual, were harder to pin down than obvious violations such as an influx of cockroaches, or prepared food left as a target for pigeon droppings when stored in a grimy back yard instead of the refrigerator.

It was hard to prove, and thus sanction, claims that the young server in a certain establishment continually scratched his bottom between serving courses, unless one was prepared to hang around for long enough to catch him in the act. Some of the reported offences were indeed outrageous, such as the instance where I was called to confirm suspicions that a cat was kept in a certain kitchen, the obvious giveaway being feline hairs in the food. My diligent investigation revealed that the chef did indeed keep a cat in the kitchen, but, as he explained, it was only until it had the mice population under control. Naturally I closed the place down until pest control could report the place was free of vermin, though after it re-opened I was subsequently forced to close it down permanently when the now idle cat was served up as the main course.

On one occasion I was called in to deal with a complaint about flagrant cross contamination of food in a sandwich shop close to Manchester's Piccadilly. Some ignoramus had purchased a sandwich before boarding the train; during his journey he ended up engrossed in a newspaper article about the dangers of cross contamination between raw and cooked food. Wasting no time he reported the sandwich shop, even going so far as lurking outside the Food Standards Agency and personally waylaying me as I left my office, accosting me with his asinine evidence. The chap clearly wasn't a full shilling, labouring under the misapprehension that cross contamination had occurred by the placement of cooked chicken next to raw bread. I patiently explained this was a common and acceptable practice in the presentation of sandwiches, but the poor fellow couldn't grasp it, insisting the bread must be raw as it hadn't been toasted.

Anyway, I digress. After years of familiarity with Scraper's stringent standards I knew he was diligent enough to spot a typo at fifty paces or latch onto an obscure numerical error in an appendix. The sheer outrage he expressed over the slightest grammatical error or an inexcusable homonym led me to believe he was pedantic enough to satisfy my need for a meticulous, nay even obsessively punctilious, editor. I hoped that Scrapes would appreciate the self-depreciating tone I had adopted when penning the book and thus resist the urge to litter the margins with references to my pomposity.

A hand on my shoulder shook me from my reverie and I realised I was neglecting my repping duties. Springing into action I grabbed the microphone, ready to impart interesting information about the terrain. I pointed out the small coastal villages below us, the particular stretch of road we were on offering panoramic views of the familiar coast. As Sakis directed the coach towards Itilo the landscape changed, transitioning from lush richness to barren hills, forbidding grey rocks creating a rather gloomy aspect. The vista could appear beyond bleak during the dark misty days of winter, but it was less foreboding in the June sunshine. I filled my charges in on some pertinent facts about the area, pointing out the old town of Itilo nestled off to one side, and the fortress of Kelefa overlooking the Bay of Limeni. As the coach hurtled down the steep hill towards Neo Itilo, the newer and sister settlement of the old town, the group exclaimed in awe at the magnificent view.

"I have a question." Referring to my checklist I quickly identified the questioner as Gordon. "You said that we'd be having lunch in a place called Gerolimenas…"

"Yes indeed, a delightful small town."

"Well you said earlier that Gerolimenas means old port, so would I be right in thinking that the Greek word for old is gero, it would make sense when you think of geriatrics, the Greek root of the word and all that."

"Actually the Greek word for old is *palaios*," I said.

"Right, so gero must be Greek for elderly then?" Gordon persisted.

"Well actually the Greek word for elderly is *ilikomenos*," I responded cautiously, wondering if it was wise to allow myself to be dragged down this particular path. My Greek may be improving at a slow and steady pace, but my knowledge of the language does not extend to its classical roots, nor can I claim to be a scholar of the language by any stretch of the imagination.

"It says here in my guide book that *leros* means sacred," another man piped up: consulting my checklist I quickly identified the troublemaker as Bruce Weldon. "According to my guide book Gerolimenas means sacred port, not old port like you told us. You need to go back to rep school and get your facts straight…"

"No, he's right, it says in my guide book it means old harbour," Gordon contradicted Bruce. "There always has to be one know-it-all who thinks he knows best, I bet you were a teacher."

"I was, I taught algebra for…"

"Give it a rest Bruce, all these nice people are trying to enjoy a lovely day out and they aren't the slightest bit interested in your boring old algebra," Bruce's wife Carole interrupted. "Victor is it, Victor is a nice young man and I am thoroughly enjoying listening to him talk. I'm certainly more interested in what he has to tell us about the area than the information you can dig up from that stuffy old guide book."

V.D. BUCKET

With Bruce firmly put in his place by his wife I sent her a grateful smile. Tickled pink that she had referred to me as a young man I made a mental note to continue to apply the Grecian 2000 and to stick to my healthy Greek diet.

Chapter 13

Stepping Back in Time

There was a collective gasp of awe as the coach ascended the perilous steep, narrow and winding road towards Vathia and the tourists caught their first glimpse of the imposing tower houses perched on the hilltop, giving the impression of a cluster of huddled brooding monoliths. Atop the rugged and untamed landscape Vathia evokes a romantic image, yet I find it most compelling during the bleakest of winter days when the area projects a powerful sense of melancholic, almost ghostly, desolation. Although I would love to experience Vathia in the midst of a lightning storm when it would be at its most starkly dramatic, I have yet to persuade Marigold to venture in that direction during thunderous weather with low visibility.

My audience had been most attentive when I gave them the potted history of the largely abandoned town that had once represented a symbol of defiance against the Ottomans. The Maniots, proud descendants of the Spartans, had a consummate history of standing firm against not only Turkish invaders and any number of marauding enemies with nefarious intentions, but also Sicilian, Venetian, Corsican, and Algerian pirates.

At the peak of its heyday in the eighteenth and nineteenth centuries the population of Vathia stood in the tens of thousands, the inhabitants holing up in fortified towers to fiercely protect their territory. When there were no ravaging invaders to repel, the Maniots maintained their reputation for fighting by battling rival clans, engaging in bitter skirmishes over scraps of arid land or matters of honour, stoking legendary feuds that became generational. In addition to fighting off foreign pirates the Maniots engaged in piracy themselves, plundering passing trade ships and hiding their stolen treasures amid the warren of pirate caves tucked away on the jagged coastline, or supplementing their income by serving as mercenaries for foreign armies.

Without the wealth of pirate plunder the inaccessible region struggled to support its population which has now dwindled down to only a handful of families in present times, the arid landscape not conducive to cultivating food. The sparse and spindly olive trees appear almost too battered by the elements to produce fruit, and the long and arduous trek through the crumbling terraces and barren scrubland to the sea far below makes fishing an unattractive proposition.

Sakis parked up and the tourists disembarked, gaping in wonder at the picture perfect image of Vathia. "It's like stepping back in time, it's almost medieval in its grandeur," Carole said.

I told her that the town was at its peak in the eighteenth century though it does have an aura of the Middle Ages. I repeated an interesting fact picked up from my studies of the area, telling my charges that the Americans had already put a man on the moon before a paved road reached the end of the Mani in the 1970s. I invited the group to roam through the village at their leisure and explore the abandoned towers, only taking care not to disturb any inhabitants still in residence. It wouldn't do for any remaining Maniots to become the objects of gawping curiosity.

"I can't believe someone hasn't taken the opportunity to renovate these towers and turn them into hotels," Gordon observed.

"I do believe that the Greek Tourist Board considered converting some of the towers into boutique hotels about twenty years ago, but nothing came of it," I said. "The lack of accessible beaches and the remoteness of the area most likely holds little appeal to the mass tourist market. I imagine the area will remain undeveloped and Vathia will continue to attract the more discerning visitor with an interest in its history."

"I can see that, and it's certainly quite wonderful to able to explore without the place being overrun with tourists," Gordon said. "We went to Monemvasia a couple of summers ago and the place was jam- packed, couldn't move without tripping over a Japanese tourist."

"Fabulous excursions like this make the Mani

an ideal holiday destination for us," Carole commented. "We like to split our days between discovering traditional sights and relaxing on the beach."

"Speak for yourself, I'd much rather have a good ruin without bothering with any beaches," Bruce said, consulting his guidebook no doubt to ensure I hadn't missed out on disclosing any pertinent facts.

The small group scattered eager to explore the shady tracks between the stone towers. I followed in their wake, never tiring of visiting this magical place. I paused beside a humongous prickly pear plant to admire the old church in the town square, the cobbled ground at my feet stained with the juice of centuries of rotted figs, the silence only broken by the persistent yelp of a dog in the distance. Climbing up a narrow steep avenue between tall tower houses I noted the moss and weeds sprouting between the crumbling stonework, wondering if an ancient wooden door hanging precariously on its hinges would creak if I pushed it or simply disintegrate beneath my touch. Looking upwards I saw the window apertures devoid of glass and imagined former occupants crouching behind them, weapons poised as they kept a wary eye on the approaching enemy or perhaps sharpening their blades for a spot of ritual decapitation.

Recalling my first visit to Vathia with Marigold and Barry, I remembered my excitement upon discovering an empty shotgun cartridge in the dirt beneath a scraggy cactus, voicing my thought that perhaps it had lain there for over a century, evidence of a rival feud. I must admit I felt rather naïve when Barry grabbed the cartridge and scoffed at my imaginings, pointing out it wasn't old at all. He said it was most likely left over from the hunting season and that someone had no doubt been taking pot shots at wild boars or quail.

When the group had finished their leisurely wanderings I called them together to show them the old olive press housed in a run-down stone building indistinguishable from the other former dwellings. Ducking through the low entrance I propped the door open, inviting the sunlight to stream into the dark room and cast its rays on the old olive implements lining the whitewashed walls. An old wooden carving with an almost bronze cast, weathered with age, depicting elaborate floral tendrils sprouting from a sculpted vase, adorned one wall, hanging at a precarious angle from a rusty nail.

Stepping into the old olive mill was like stepping back in time. The centre of the floor was dominated by a fabulous deep stone basin forming the base of the olive press, a gnarled yet solid wooden beam attached to a huge stone millstone used to grind the olives. In olden times a donkey, or strong men, would manipulate the wooden handle in an endless circuitous route, the metal axis grinding rhythmically in tune with the repetitive labour.

"Unfortunately the modern local presses aren't operational at this time of year, but if you do visit Greece out of season I'd recommend you call into one and compare it to this ancient press," I suggested.

"It's all so wonderful, this excursion is definitely the highlight of my holiday," Carole gushed.

The group all appeared to have thoroughly enjoyed the stop at Vathia, but the rumbling of stomachs reminded me it was time for lunch. For once I didn't need to round up any stragglers as we boarded the coach since there seemed to be a cumulative desire to get stuck into traditional roast goat.

My tourist charges chorused their approval when

we pulled into the coastal retreat of Gerolimenos, the sea a welcome sight in the midst of the desolate scrubby and stone strewn landscape. The small town nestling below the steep bank of Cavo Grosso was established as a thriving trading port in the late nineteenth century, soon becoming famous for the export of quails to Marseilles. The importance of the port has long since waned, Gerolimenos now little more than a picturesque back-water, well off the tourist trail.

Aged stone buildings surrounding the port drew comments of admiration as we made our way to the restaurant overlooking the water. Half-a-dozen octopuses were suspended from a flimsy washing line at the edge of the water, their pinkish mottled tentacles drying out in the sunshine. Ducking below the catch of the day we headed to the two water-side tables reserved for our group, shaded beneath deep blue sun umbrellas mirroring the colour of the sea; giant earthenware pots brimming with scented geraniums adding a splash of colourful cheer. Recalling that I had slipped my new Polaroid shades into my top pocket, I swapped them out with my regular sunglasses, amazed by the way they accentuated the colours, transforming the calm blue sea into the deepest turquoise. I was delighted that Marigold had persuaded me to splash out on the stylish shades, even though I had cynically attributed her badgering me into buying them as a cunning distraction from her own extravagant splurge on the latest must-have fashion in sunglasses.

The restaurant was adjacent to the narrow pebble beach abutting the main street running through the village. A typical blue and white fishing boat was moored on the beach; a weather-beaten old fisherman wrapped up in a long sleeved shirt and a thick pullover despite the heat was engrossed in untangling his nets, a tatty straw hat shielding his face from the sun.

The group settled in at the two tables, some of the party eager to bag seats next to Sakis and me. "I have to say that sort of simple life holds a lot of appeal," Gordon said, nodding towards the fisherman.

"Simple but hard," I said. "Up before dawn and out long beyond midnight, braving the elements at sea."

"Have you ever eaten octopus, Victor?" Carole asked, shuddering at the sight of the suspended molluscs. "I don't believe I'd be brave enough to try it."

"It really is most delicious," I assured her. "I especially enjoy it when it has been slightly charred on an outdoor grill, but my wife prefers it as a cold appetiser in vinegar."

"I'm feeling adventurous. Do you suppose I could swap the goat for octopus?" Gordon piped up.

"I'm afraid our set menu doesn't extend to octopus, anything fished out of the sea tends to be a tad pricey," I said just as Andreas, the restaurant owner, began to plonk plates of aromatic roast goat down on the table. Overhearing the exchange Andreas laughed, explaining to the group, "When I was the young the meat is the luxury and we eat every day the fishes we catch, now the fishes is the luxury, even the fishermen can to only afford to eat it for the special holiday like the *Pascha*."

"Easter," I helpfully translated.

As Andreas shuffled back to the kitchen to fetch more plates, Fiona, one of the tourists sharing our table, looked down at her food, her face a study in confusion. "I can't eat this, I'm a vegetarian," she announced.

"Did you tick the vegetarian option when you signed up for the trip?" I enquired, wondering if the office had made a blunder that would result in Fiona handing in a critical customer satisfaction survey.

"I didn't notice one…" Fiona admitted.

"*Ti leei?*" Sakis hissed, sensing trouble in the air as he asked me what Fiona had said.

"*Einai chortofagos, den borei na faei katsika.*"

Hearing that Fiona was a vegetarian who wouldn't eat goat Sakis raised his eyebrows, leaning over and forking the roast meat from Fiona's plate and replacing it with the artichokes from his own lunch.

"How kind," Fiona gushed, beaming with pleasure, seemingly not at all worried by the goat juices contaminating her now vegetarian lunch.

"*Tipota,*" Sakis mumbled through a mouthful of goat, careful to keep his eyes down in case his generous gesture encouraged unwanted flirting.

Conversation flowed as we tucked into our tasty lunch, Carole settling on a topic I was all too familiar with during my repping trips.

"I must say I do admire your bravery in upsticking to a foreign country. We've often talked about doing it ourselves but it isn't practical with our situation, Bruce's mother is widowed and we need to pop in regularly and collect her shopping."

There was a visible age difference between Carole and her grumpy husband Bruce who looked as though he wouldn't see his eightieth birthday again. I supposed his mother must be a centenarian.

"I'm considering converting our downstairs storage room into a granny flat and importing my mother for part of the year. She could avoid the worst of the winter weather back in England," I said.

"How thoughtful, what a devoted son you must be," Carole said, her words stinging a little when it struck me that I had rather neglected Violet Burke of late. I made a mental note to surprise her with a plane ticket to Greece very soon. I realised I would need to make a real effort to start buttering up Marigold if I was going to sell her on the idea of installing my mother in the downstairs storage space.

"I have to say this goat is top-notch, tastes just like lamb," Bruce said, somewhat mellowed from the wine that accompanied the food. "You should get the recipe Carole; it would make a nice change for our Sunday lunch back home."

"I'm not sure that goat is readily available in Tesco," Carole replied.

"The artichoke hearts bottled in oil and vinegar that I buy in Waitrose just aren't a patch on these fresh ones," Fiona sighed wistfully.

"Fresh artichokes are as cheap as chips on the market but awfully fiddly to prepare," I said. "I did have a go at growing them in the garden, but they were a magnet for snails. Of course the effort wasn't a complete waste; it saved me going out on a snail hunt. The chap who helps me out in the garden ended up feeding the artichoke plants to his rabbit."

"Oh, as a vegetarian the thought of snails crawling all over the artichokes has rather made me lose my appetite," Fiona said, eyeing the vegetable on her fork suspiciously before returning it to her plate. I found her repugnance strange since she'd had no qualms about tucking into the artichokes that had been marinated in goat juices, but then again I often find vegetarians to be a tad illogical.

"I rather thought eating snails was just a Frenchie thing. I say, it was a bit of a come down for them to lose out to Greece in the football," Gordon said. The mention of football was received with indifference by the party of history buffs.

"Are the Greeks partial to eating snails?"

Carole asked.

"Indeed, foraging for food is a traditional Greek pastime," I told her, expanding the theme by regaling the table with tales of my elderly neighbours foraging for wild asparagus and *horta*, even dropping in an amusing anecdote about Sampaguita frying up grasshoppers.

As usual Sakis ate in silence, maintaining the pretence he didn't understand English, a precaution he exercised to keep any flirtatious tourists at arm's length. Mopping up the last of the lemony goat juices with crusty bread Sakis winked at me, adopting a scoffing tone when he said, *"Eisai gematos Victor, trogontas pragmati salinkaria. Argotera pairno ti fili mou se Goodies yia grigoro fagito."*

Although I didn't translate his words for the benefit of those at our table despite their quizzical looks, for the benefit of the reader Sakis said "You're full of it Victor, eating snails indeed. Later I will take my girlfriend to Goody's for fast food."

Leaning in I whispered to Sakis that although he may scoff, tourist appreciation for my casual chatter about snails and *horta* would be reflected in the tips we received later.

Chapter 14

Caught on Camera

Cynthia dozed all the way home, only stirring as we reached the outskirts of Meli when I was forced to slam on the brakes to avoid colliding with the back of Panos' tractor. The tractor's creeping pace prevented me from overtaking and Cynthia sighed in irritation at this last minute delay. Pulling off into one of his fields, Panos waved cheerily and Cynthia exhaled in relief, excited at the prospect of soon being reunited with the baby.

"Victor, I forgot to ask, I need an enormous favour. The new rep Terry has let me down at the last moment and he can't do the authentic Greek village taverna experience tomorrow evening. I know it is terribly short notice…"

"I did warn you he appeared unreliable."

"I should have listened to you. Anyway he's rather left me in the lurch; I wouldn't ask if I wasn't desperate. You know how popular the evening is," Cynthia wheedled.

"I'd really rather not. You know I don't rep at nights Cynthia, I have always been resolute on that point," I objected. I'd had quite enough of working unsociable hours during the winter I had cheffed in Nikos' taverna.

"I'll have to do it myself then, but I just can't bear the thought of leaving Anastasia at bedtime." A pitiful sob rounded off Cynthia's words and her pleading tone stirred some sympathy in me; I felt myself weakening. The taverna involved was one I hadn't actually visited yet and I was quite keen to try it out, though preferably not in the company of a coachload of tourists seeking a genuine Greek experience. Sensing my hesitation Cynthia added, "The food is supposed to be really excellent and you'll get a free meal of course."

BUCKET TO GREECE (VOL. 6)

"Can I take Barry along with me?" I asked thinking at least it would give him an excuse to escape the clutches of the terrible Trouts.

"Of course, I'm sure he'd love to join you, having my parents around is making him crabby. I'll let the taverna know to prepare an extra plate. I really do appreciate it Victor."

"Just this once Cynthia, don't go expecting it to be regular thing. It's a good job it doesn't involve any research."

"No research required at all Victor," Cynthia assured me before dropping her bombshell. "I'm sure you'll be a natural leading the Greek dancing and smashing a few plates."

I assumed an expression of complete diffidence, refusing to give Cynthia the satisfaction of letting her know I was aware that she had well and truly suckered me in.

As I parked the Punto in the village square Cynthia was practically clamping at the bit to rush home and see Anastasia.

"You hurry in to the baby, I'll bring in your bags of detergent from the boot," I offered. I must confess my gesture was not entirely altruistic; I never could pass up an opportunity to cuddle my exceedingly cute niece.

Following Cynthia indoors it struck me that the house was unnaturally quiet. I hoped that Anastasia wasn't napping or I would miss my chance to cosy up with the adorable little bundle. There was no sign of life, or any of the usual baby paraphernalia cluttering up the downstairs rooms. Cynthia came hurtling down the stairs, hysterically calling out "Anastasia isn't here. What has my mother done with the baby?"

"The pram isn't here, she's probably taken Anastasia out for a walk around the village," I suggested. "Let me just check if there's anyone out back."

Stepping outside I immediately spotted Anne Trout sprawled out on a sun lounger by the side of the ecological pond, a glass of wine in her hand and a bottle beside her. She appeared to have made a remarkable recovery from her avowed aversion to frogs. Cynthia, hot on my heels, squealed in shock. "What are you doing, what have you done with my baby?"

The Trout woman lowered her sunglasses and peered peevishly at her daughter. Immediately on the defensive she retorted "Don't take that tone with me, Cynthia. Surely you don't begrudge me a glass of wine and a spot of sunbathing when I've spent a long and exhausting day babysitting for you? Have you any idea how gruelling it is caring for a baby in this heat? I really would have expected you to demonstrate a bit of gratitude instead of taking that accusatory tone."

"I'm sorry mother, I just panicked; of course I appreciate you babysitting…"

"I should think so too; I am supposed to be on holiday you know. You have no idea what an absolute slog it was to get out here to this remote place. Why you couldn't have settled down in Cheshire I'll never know, you do always have to be so contrary."

Listening to this exchange I bridled on Cynthia's behalf, noticing she was too cowed to stand up to her mother. Looking around as though expecting to see the pram parked in the shade, Cynthia suddenly unleashed a desperate cry "But where is my baby? Where is Anastasia?"

"Oh for goodness sake, there's no need to get unhinged Cynthia, get a grip. Why not sit down and join me in a nice glass of wine, but first go and see if you can rustle up any nibbles in the kitchen. Some pistachios would complement the wine nicely. I'm a bit peckish because you didn't bother to leave me any lunch, very thoughtless of you Cynthia; you know I can't be expected to get along in a strange Greek kitchen. Chop chop girl, grab some nuts. It's another hour until we have to be at that dinner party," Anne Trout ordered in the most condescending tone.

Ignoring her mother's demand for nuts Cynthia quietly asked "Has Dad taken my baby out for a walk?"

"I think your father went for a walk in the village, and the baby…" she paused as though trying to remember what she had done with Anastasia. "Ah yes, the baby is having a nice visit with her other grandmother."

"You are Anastasia's only grandmother," Cynthia said woodenly.

"That red haired woman, oh yes, Barry's sister, Marjorie," Anne Trout said as though the slight matter of the baby's whereabouts was of absolutely no concern.

Appalled by Anne Trout's insensitivity towards her daughter I gripped Cynthia by the arm and led her back inside. "Come on Cynthia, I'll drive you to ours," I said, firing a parting shot over my shoulder. "It's Marigold, not Marjorie, I'd advise you to get her name right when you turn up for our dinner party later."

BUCKET TO GREECE (VOL. 6)

* * *

"There you are Victor, thank goodness you're home. You need to get started chopping the beetroot for the *pantzarosalata*, I'm all behind. Oh, hello Cynthia," Marigold trilled as we entered the kitchen. Cynthia immediately dashed over to scoop up Anastasia who was cooing away sweetly in her pram.

"The beetroot, Victor," Marigold continued oblivious to Cynthia's relief in finding the baby in such capable hands. "I managed to gut the fish for the soup but I did get rather behind with the dinner party preparations, Anastasia is the most delicious distraction but I rather expected that Anne would have been back over to collect her by now."

"I rather panicked when Anastasia wasn't at home with my mother," Cynthia said. "She promised to babysit for the day. How long has the baby been over here Marigold?"

"Well let me see, it was well before my elevenses. Anne said she had something very important to do and of course I never mind watching little Anastasia, you know how I love to have her. But with the dinner party to prepare I've rather had my hands full."

"And she hasn't been back since this morning?" Cynthia said.

"No, it's a bit odd when I come to think of it. But then again she did have something important on."

"Sunbathing and necking wine can hardly be considered matters of monumental importance," I snapped in irritation, recalling that Anne Trout had assured Cynthia that she had been babysitting all day. Really Cynthia's parents struck me as not only a pair of irresponsible and reluctant grandparents, but lazy ones too.

"I'll just gather all the baby things together and take Anastasia home," Cynthia said.

"You may as well just stay put now that you're here, everyone will be arriving for the dinner party soon," Marigold said. "Give Barry a ring and tell him to come straight here from work."

"Would you mind awfully if we give it a miss, Marigold? After a day back at work I just want to spend the evening at home with Barry and the baby."

"Of course, I didn't consider how exhausted you must be after working all day. Just take a seat and I'll box up some salad and soup for you to take home to save you cooking," Marigold offered.

"Oh that's so thoughtful of you Marigold; I'm really dead on my feet and it will be such a relief not to cook."

"I'm not surprised after a full day of working in this heat, not to mention the long drive up to town and back," Marigold cooed sympathetically. "Victor, dig out a couple of Tupperware bowls and fill them with food for Cynthia, there's soup in the pan and salad in the fridge. I made plenty."

"In case it escaped your notice I have been working all day too," I pointed out in exasperation.

"Really Victor, you do exaggerate, I'm sure that you spent most of your day either sitting around eating a free lunch or relaxing on the coach. You have no consideration of how difficult it was to spend all day babysitting while preparing for a dinner party, it wasn't exactly a piece of cake," Marigold retorted.

"Yes dear," I replied meekly. There were times when arguing with my wife was simply futile and I recognised this as one of them. Just then the telephone rang.

"Do get that Victor," Marigold instructed. "I do hope it isn't someone cancelling at the last moment, so inconsiderate."

I was surprised to hear the caller was Tina from the village shop. After listening in shock to what Tina had to tell me I simply told Marigold I needed to attend to something urgently, not bothering to elaborate.

"But Victor, the beetroot..." Marigold's cry of exasperation rang in my ears as I rushed out of the house, running slap bang into Barry as I reached the street.

"Victor, can you believe that ghastly Trout woman has farmed Anastasia out to Marigold? She's sitting out by the pond like Lady Muck, chucking pistachios at the frogs. Cynthia is going to be so upset when she finds out her mother couldn't be bothered to babysit as she promised," Barry said, barely able to control his anger.

"Hold on Barry, Cynthia is upstairs with the baby but we have a more pressing matter to deal with. Come on, I'll fill you in on the way to the shop," I said, dragging him along by the arm.

When we arrived in the shop Tina threw her hands in the air in a dramatic gesture I was unable to interpret. *"Victor, Barry, ti boro na kano, sas efcharisto pou irthate,"* the shopkeeper rattled off at speed. It was quite surprising to hear Tina say 'what can I do, thank you for coming,' in Greek. Usually she is almost religious in her insistence on practicing her English on us. "*Skeftome na kaleso tin astynomia, alla tote nomizo oti o anthropos einai syngenis sas.*"

"Did you get all that?" Barry hissed. "The only word I caught was police."

"I'm sure she said something about wanting to call the police, but then she realised the man is related to us."

"The man?" Barry repeated, shaking his head in confusion as Tina ushered us into her back storeroom, leaving her young niece Thalia in charge of the shop. The teenager was staying with her aunt in Meli for a couple of weeks to give her parents a break during the seemingly interminable thirteen week school holidays. Thalia barely looked up as we slipped behind the counter, engrossed in zapping some pesky electronic aliens on her Game Boy.

"Lester," Barry and I parroted in surprised unison upon discovering Barry's father-in-law sitting on a hard backed chair in the dimly lit storeroom, an expression of outrage plastered on his features. His face was unnaturally puce and his persistent twitch exacerbated the sense of frustrated anger seeping from him. As my eyes grew accustomed to the gloomy light I gasped in utter shock when I realised that Lester wasn't willingly sitting on the chair at all, but was in fact bound in place, struggling against a rope secured tightly around his waist.

"*Ti symvainei sti gi, yiati einai demenos?*" I cried out, demanding to know what on earth was going on and why Tina had Lester tied to the chair.

"*Koita ti prospathise na klepse,*" Tina replied, her hand sweeping over a half-dozen bars of *ION sokolata*, the iconic Greek brand of traditional chocolate with almonds, as she informed us that Lester had tried to steal them. The very notion that Lester had pocketed the confectionary without paying for it left me reeling; if Tina had indeed caught Lester red-handed then he was nothing short of a common shoplifter.

"Look I've no idea what this madwoman is saying but tell her to untie me at once," Lester demanded, straining futilely against the rope. "Doesn't she realise that I'm British?"

There was something about Lester's arrogant tone that instinctively rubbed me up the wrong way. Ignoring the captive man I turned to Tina. "You really saw him stealing…" I began to say before realising that Tina was perhaps too overwrought to cope with translating my words. Switching to Greek I repeated my words. "*Eisai sigouros oti ekleve?*" speaking loudly to drown out Lester's strident cries that we free him.

"*Nai, nai, eimai sigouros, eimai sigouros.*" Tina assured me she was sure. Taking a deep breath she said in measured English, "Thalia watch him, she see all. That girl never miss anything, he have the eye like the vulture."

"Hawk," I automatically corrected, whilst letting the inaccurate gender slip. About to say more, I held my tongue as several scenarios raced through my mind. Perchance Thalia was indeed hawk-eyed, though each time I had been in the shop recently she had appeared totally preoccupied with her Game Boy. I certainly was not prepared to condemn Lester on the say-so of a possibly unreliable teenager who may have let her vivid imagination run away with her. Perhaps Thalia was exacting some petty revenge on Lester because he had been deliberately condescending or rude to her, or perhaps Thalia had mistaken Lester for a seedy pervert who was winking inappropriately at the tender-aged girl, ignorant that he suffered from an involuntary twitch. Having been on the receiving end of Lester's unfortunate manner I leapt to the conclusion that Lester had offended Thalia or twitched at her once too often, and she was throwing false accusations at him to make him squirm.

"Barry, I insist you untie me at once, that madwoman needs locking up," Lester shouted.

"It is the good the security camera see him to put the chocolate in the, how you say in English, the pocket," Tina added, shattering the convenient excuse I had concocted for the thief.

"There's a security camera," Lester stuttered, his eyes swivelling manically between the three of us. "What will I do? Anne will go ballistic if this gets out."

"You were stealing bars of chocolate?" Barry accused, making no attempt to conceal the contempt in his voice.

"I didn't mean to, I just gave into temptation. Anne wouldn't give me any pocket money," Lester blubbed, tears rolling from one eye whilst its twitching partner remained bizarrely dry.

"Look Tina, I'll pay for the chocolate and I would be most grateful if you don't summon the police. Perhaps you could just ban Lester from the shop instead," I suggested.

"Ban, I not to understand…"

Tina looked none the wiser when Barry said "you can bar him."

"*Min ton afisete sto magazi*," I translated.

"*Entaxei*, I no want to call the police. It is the bad to see the police to take away the family," Tina said, her face suffused in an involuntary blush that made me surmise Marigold's assertion that Tina had called the police on her own mother, Despina, for illegal Sunday trading, was true. Tina's blush, coupled with her reluctance to call the police on Lester, led me to believe she felt guilty for having her own mother arrested, even though it had served a useful purpose.

"*Efcharistoume* Tina, thank you for your discretion," I said.

"It is the right thing to do. You have the good name in the village," Tina said. I was touched by her words.

"Cynthia will be so grateful, she'd never live it down if her father was arrested as a common thief," Barry added.

"I rather think Cynthia has got enough on her plate, perhaps best all round if we don't mention this," I suggested.

"Oh please, please don't tell Anne or Cynthia..." Lester begged. His words trailed off into gibberish and he squirmed in fear, his eyes bulging out of his head as Tina approached him with a knife saying "*meine akinitos*."

"Stop her, don't let her stab me. I promise I will never steal anything again."

"Shut up and keep still you idiot, she's telling you not to move while she cuts you free," I said.

Whilst Tina hacked at the rope with the blunt knife, Barry pulled me to one side, saying "I think you're right, best if Cynthia doesn't hear about this, best if we can keep this whole sorry business between ourselves. It wouldn't look good if word got around that I was related to a criminal, not with people trusting me to work in their homes."

Nodding in agreement I felt embarrassment course through my body; after all Barry wasn't the only one related to a criminal, though in this instance Barry's connection was only a loose one through marriage. My own criminal connection was much closer to home as I had been fathered by an actual fraudster who had served prison time. Ever since I had accidentally attended my father's funeral I had been racked with subliminal shame that I was spawned by a man of dubious character, at the same time trying to convince myself it had no bearing on the man I had grown into. Having never committed a criminal act in my life I can hardly be held responsible for any vile acts perpetrated by a relative stranger. Equally Cynthia should not suffer her name being besmirched through association and I resolved to go out of my way to protect the good name of my sister-in-law. Lester being caught in the act had put my own situation in perspective and strangely freed me from the guilt I had been carrying. The weight I had carried lifted; I felt vindicated.

Looking Barry directly in the eye I assured him "Neither Cynthia or you can in any way be held responsible for what your vile relatives get up to. If word does get out about Lester's petty thievery you must both hold your heads up high, neither of you have anything to feel ashamed about."

"That means a lot coming from you Victor," Barry said.

"Now let's put our heads together and see if we can't turn this to our advantage. I'm not above using a bit of blackmail on Lester; we can promise to keep schtum and not say a word to

Anne if he promises to pack their bags and clear off."

Chapter 15

All the Latest Fashions

"Really Victor, what could possibly have been so important that you had to dash off without seeing to the beetroot?" Marigold griped when I returned home.

"I needed something from the shop," I replied, transfixed by the gruesome sight of my wife's crimson hands. It appeared as though she had dipped them in a bucket of blood, but luckily, since there was no bloodied corpse littering the kitchen floor, I deduced they were simply stained bright red from the beetroot juices.

V.D. BUCKET

"Well it's odd that you've returned empty handed then," Marigold observed with a withering look. Being nobody's fool my wife could sense something was amiss, but with guests due to arrive at any moment she sensibly decided to brush it under the carpet. No doubt the matter would receive a suitable airing at bedtime.

"Really Marigold, we have an ample supply of disposable gloves," I chided, selecting a lemon and slicing it in half. "Hold your hands out over the sink," I instructed, squeezing the juice over her fingers and adding a teaspoonful of coarse sea salt to cleanse them.

Although I am not in the habit of keeping secrets from my wife, in this instance I felt discretion was the best course of action, at least until the dinner party was out of the way. Marigold would be mortified if she knew we were about to give house room to a common shoplifter and would spend a fraught evening keeping an eye on our best silver, figuratively speaking of course. The thought of entertaining Anne and Lester Trout in our home did not sit well with me, but if I disinvited them at this late hour I would be forced to fill Marigold in on recent events: she certainly wouldn't appreciate her mood being ruined just before she was due to play the role of scintillating hostess.

"I'm just off for a quick shower; it wouldn't do to receive guests in my repping uniform," I said.

"Can you just winch the bucket up first?"

Since we often dined on the roof terrace we had found it a terrible inconvenience to continually troop up and down the hazardous stone steps with our hands full of crockery and cutlery. Barry had recently suggested the ingenious yet simple solution of creating the poor man's version of a dumbwaiter. Unfortunately he had been so busy with his own home renovations, work, and the baby that he hadn't had time to implement his novel idea of installing a winch on the roof terrace and attaching it to a receptacle which could be lowered to the kitchen window and filled with the necessary accoutrements for dining atop. Even though I am not renowned for my DIY skills I deduced this was a job I could easily tackle myself by substituting a hand cranked winch for a rope tied to the terrace railings and attached to a bucket. Now all we needed to do was fill the bucket with the items needed to lay the table and yank it upwards.

"You load the bucket and I'll pull it up before I jump in the shower," I agreed.

The terrace floor was littered with a delicate covering of lilac wisteria petals, evoking romantic images of confetti thrown at a wedding. I noted that the wisteria growing up the side of the house was in desperate need of a good pruning, its upper branches entangled in the ornate railings surrounding the terrace perimeter. I made a mental note to add giving the wisteria a good haircut to Guzim's to-do list.

"Throw a dustpan and brush in the bucket," I called down to my wife. I chuckled to myself imagining perhaps making a small fortune by patenting the ingenious bucket on a rope set-up and selling it to my Greek neighbours who had likely never come across the concept of a dumbwaiter. It could be money for old rope. I supposed that without Barry's technical winch the idea wasn't novel enough to sell, but it really saved a lot of wasted energy in repeated trips up the hazardous stone staircase.

Refreshed from my shower I joined Marigold in the kitchen as she put the finishing touches to the evening's spread.

"I forgot to tell you, I had a lovely chat with Sampaguita. I told her how much she is needed in Meli, with Cynthia needing a hand with the baby whilst she's working and Giannis' grandfather desperate for some home help in Nektar."

"Did you manage to persuade her to return to Meli rather than look for a new job in Athens?" I asked, cringing at the thought of how much that particular long distance phone call would set me back.

"Let's just say she dropped the idea of Athens when I told her how much Spiros is missing her and that he is a shadow of his former self without her. She is going to fly back to Greece next week and accept the work in Meli," Marigold said. "It appears that her reluctance to return really stemmed from a few disapproving and malicious comments that she overheard in the shop, painting her as a gold digger trying to land herself a rich Greek husband. I'm afraid she rather took them to heart, especially as Spiros had just inherited another house."

"Meddling gossips, I would love to bang all their heads together," I said. "It is as clear as day that Spiros and Sampaguita are besotted with one another. I must just give Spiros a quick call to let him know…"

"Tell him to phone her with a bit of sweet talk…I'm sure she'd be overjoyed if he met her flight." Marigold beamed with pleasure, delighted her Cupid intervention had gone down so well. I was sure that Spiros would propose once Sampaguita was back in the village. I made a mental note to advise Violet Burke to be on the lookout for a new hat in the summer sales; my mother has a real weakness for hats and she is sure to want to attend Sampaguita's wedding since a certain fondness has developed between the old battle-axe and the fragrant Filipana.

I placed a quick call to Spiros. He was indeed so elated to hear the news of Sampaguita's imminent return that he instructed me to 'give to the Marigold a kiss.' Marigold graciously received the kiss by proxy, relieved not to be overpowered by Spiros' aftershave.

As the guests began to arrive I herded everyone onto the balcony for a glass of wine since it made no sense to troop up to the roof terrace until everyone was gathered. Milton and Edna, and Doreen and Norman, arrived together, followed by Sherry, her presence somewhat awkward since she turned up without her husband in tow. I could only imagine how much havoc that would create for Marigold's carefully thought out seating plan.

Sherry and Felix were relatively new British arrivals to Meli, having recently purchased an old house that had been shuttered for years. Barry and Vangelis had been retained to do the renovation work, a job they regretted taking on almost as soon as their quote was accepted. The house was perched at the top of a steep track that was too narrow and stony to allow access by van, forcing the two men to cart all the necessary materials and tools by hand. I liked to quip that if they'd had any foresight they would have invested in a suitable ass to do the donkey work.

Felix micromanaged the budget for the job, demanding an accounting of all expenditure at the end of each working day, whilst Sherry micromanaged the builders, pestering them with endless suggestions and never allowing them a single moment of peace. Her unrelenting enthusiasm for the project was not so much contagious as exhausting, so much that Barry complained her 'jolly-hockey-sticks school headmistress cheerleading from the side-lines' approach was suffocating.

"That Sherry just doesn't know when to put a sock in it. We can't even have a frappé in peace without her expecting us to enthuse over her latest mood board," Barry had moaned at me more than once whilst he was on the job. "Course that husband of hers has the right idea; he clears off every day, and goes off walking all kitted out in absurd safari gear. He rolls up just when we're getting ready to leave for the day, delaying us while he puts the kibosh on whatever extravagant décor plans Sherry has dreamt up to put a spoke in his budget."

Vangelis, a man noted for his patience and good-humour, was at the end of his tether long before the job was finished. Joining in with Barry's complaints he sank his head in his hands, groaning "I have spend the more time with the Sherry than I have with the Athena in nearly thirty years of marry. The Sherry is the spike in my side; I cannot to turn round without the tripping over her, always with the teeth out in that, how to say in English…"

"Horsey smile," I suggested.

"Horse? What has the horse to do, no, how to say in English, *masela*?" Vangelis queried.

"False teeth," I supplied.

"She's too full-on if you ask me. She's nothing better to do with her time than constantly nit-pick even though she's likely never wielded a paintbrush in her pampered life," Barry had concurred. "It's just not natural for anyone to be so hyper all the time."

BUCKET TO GREECE (VOL. 6)

"Perhaps she's medicated," I suggested.

"Hardly, we get a well-meaning lecture about overdosing on caffeine every time we dare to stop for a frappé. It's no wonder Felix disappears every day to escape her."

With the work on their house now almost completed Marigold told me that the couple were eager to throw themselves wholeheartedly into the ex-pat scene, a scene I would most definitely go out of my way to avoid if it was not for the small matter of placating my wife. Marigold had duly invited them to her dinner party this evening, hoping they would blend naturally into the mix. Because Felix had spent all his days putting as much possible distance between himself and his wife with his endless walks, and Shelly had barely had chance to leave the house since she had no faith in the workmen to manage without her obsessive micromanagement, the couple were barely beyond nodding acquaintance with any of the locals.

"Felix flew back to England last Sunday," Sherry revealed when Marigold commented on his absence. "He couldn't stand much more of the heat, he said it was getting much too hot for walking."

"And you stayed on without him, I say that's

a bit daring, going it alone in a foreign country without your husband," Milton observed. The local purveyor of porn had only just been introduced to Sherry: fortunately he had managed to refrain from mentioning her name mirrored that of one of his raunchy characters. Personally I'm of the opinion that Milton's predilection for naming his characters after alcoholic beverages displays a distinct lack of imagination that does not bode well for his future career as a writer. I even have my suspicions that Milton stooped to a spot of plagiarism; it is no secret that we named our chickens after drinks.

"Good grief, Felix isn't my husband, whatever made you think that?" Sherry brayed loudly, throwing her head back to expose a set of horsey dentures.

Milton broke the rather uncomfortable silence: "Well living in sin is all the rage now, none of our business if you tied the knot or not. I think you'll find that we're all broad minded out here, what."

"Oh no, you've got completely the wrong end of the stick, Felix is my step-son." Shelly's statement was met with shocked silence. "Felix has been an absolute rock since Henry died, insisting on coming over to Greece with me to sort out all the paperwork when I decided to move over here. Henry left strict instructions for Felix to oversee my inheritance; he was so worried I wouldn't be able to manage my finances without Felix's guidance. I'm so lucky to have my step-son to keep me in line, being an accountant he's the perfect man for the job, especially as I'm such a silly dolt when it comes to money. Henry took care of all that side of things, I've never so much as written a cheque or paid a bill in my life."

I remembered running into Felix one morning and engaging in a brief conversation that didn't touch on anything personal. Felix had confided he was a keen walker, recommending a little track he had discovered that meandered through the olive terraces and cut down to the coast from Meli. It struck me that it had been only natural to assume that Felix and Sherry were a couple; his appearance led me to believe he was perhaps ten years Sherry's senior so it was quite a surprise to learn he was in fact her step-son. Putting two and two together I concluded that the deceased Henry must have been an octogenarian at the very least; likely he had taken a much younger trophy wife, a conclusion borne out by Shelly's free admittance of her financial naivety.

"Very brave of you to move to foreign parts as a widow," Milton said.

"I've always loved Greece. Henry indulged me with holidays over here, but he flatly refused to even consider emigrating. Felix was very supportive of my move and of course it gives him the perfect base for walking. The only things Felix gets passionate about are his stuffy old ledgers and his walks; he can combine both when he visits to look over my accounts," Shelly brayed.

"So what made you decide on Meli, it's a bit out of the way?" Marigold asked.

"That was part of the attraction; it's so easy for one to become isolated in large towns whereas small villages allow one to blend into the fabric of the local society. When the estate agent told me there was a thriving ex-pat community in Meli it was the icing on the cake."

"The estate agent?" I queried.

"Sven, a lovely Nordic fellow," Shelly said.

Marigold and I exchanged bemused glances. We both remembered the pushy Nordic estate agent we had ditched before fortuitously meeting Spiros. It didn't surprise me that Sven would resort to underhand methods to flog a property; describing the small group of Brits who lived in Meli as a thriving ex-pat community definitely struck me as an underhand exaggeration.

"I'm just brimming with exciting ideas for some jolly events we can organise to fill up our time," Shelly guffawed. "We don't want to turn into the sort of ex-pats who don't get involved with local things."

Realisation dawned that the 'we' she referred to was the ex-pats she hoped to befriend in Meli. Considering the merry widow had only been resident in Greece for a couple of months I found her remark to be more than a tad patronising. I for one had no desire to be roped into any jolly organised events or feel obliged to invite the woman to tag along.

Rolling her eyes at me Marigold hissed "She's had all week to mention she wasn't bringing a husband, but didn't bother; it's going to play havoc with my seating arrangements."

I imagined it would. I recalled Cynthia telling me that there had been some reluctance to include her in the group when she was still a single woman. Until she took up with Barry she was often excluded, some of the women deluding themselves that any single woman who happened along may find their husbands desirable.

I had it on good authority, well Marigold's gossiping, that Doreen was more than a tad worried that Norman may be considered a tasty titbit to be snapped up by some predatory unattached woman. Such an absurd notion made me wonder if Doreen actually paid any attention to her husband; surely she must have noticed he has about as much charisma as a bowl of day-old porridge.

"Just don't stick me next to Norman," I hissed to Marigold, dreading the prospect of being regaled with yet more tedious facts about thermoplastic traffic cones. I felt a tad miffed that Felix wouldn't be making up the numbers: on the occasion I had bumped into him in the village he had struck me as an educated man I could get along with, certainly more my cup of tea than Norman.

"I can't think where the Trouts have got to," Marigold hissed. "The beetroot will go all soggy if they don't turn up soon."

"Oh what a delightful cat, I take it that it's a stray you rescued. Not many people would willingly take on a crippled cat," Sherry gushed approvingly when Catastrophe poked her head round the balcony.

"Actually she's a pedigree, not a stray, and

we prefer to refer to Catastrophe as differently-abled rather than crippled," Marigold protested, clearly affronted on the cat's behalf.

"And she recovered her balance amazingly well after her caudectomy," I added.

"Caudectomy, is that something Greek?" Sherry asked.

"It's the medical jargon for a partial tail amputation. Poor Catastrophe was shot by Kostis; he's a tad trigger happy and mistook the cat for a nuisance pole cat," I explained.

"Oh how terrible, we must group together and protest against all forms of hunting," Sherry said earnestly.

"Good luck with that, some of the Greeks are quite keen on their shooting and won't welcome foreign interference," I said, beginning to understand why Barry and Vangelis had found Sherry to be a tad full on.

"But surely you must support a ban on hunting? It's so terribly cruel," Sherry insisted.

"It is not my place to interfere with local culture. You might change your tune on hunting if you encounter a wild boar rummaging through the bins," I said.

"Oh, I hadn't realised that was likely. Have you run into many wild boars on the loose here in Meli?"

Just tame bores like Norman I thought to myself as Edna piped up, "We had a bit of a problem with a stubborn sheep."

"Ah, the Trouts have arrived, you can start showing everyone up to the roof terrace Victor," Marigold said when Barry's in-laws finally deigned to show up. Anne Trout must have confused our little soiree with an invitation to dine at the Ritz, her elegant cocktail dress so completely out of place that even Marigold was hard pressed to stifle an involuntary gasp. Nevertheless Marigold played the role of perfect hostess, complimenting Anne on her gorgeous dress. My wife bit her tongue when the Trout woman commented no one had warned her that the dress code for the evening was shabby and unstylish. The only tell-tale sign of Marigold's annoyance was a slight reddening of her face.

"Take no notice, you look lovely in that dress," I whispered to my wife.

"It's from the latest line at Marks and Spencer," Marigold hissed. "How on earth is she going to manage the hazardous stone staircase in those impossibly high heels? She'd better not try suing us if she turns an ankle."

"Best shove the cats in the spare room," I

suggested, thinking it could be lethal if they got underfoot.

As I led the way to the rooftop table a quick sleight of hand allowed me to craftily rearrange the place cards, putting Norman between Lester and Milton in defiance of Marigold's seating preference of girl-boy-girl. Desperate to ensure a suitable distance between myself and Norman I only realised at the last moment that I had inadvertently boxed myself in between Sherry and Anne Trout. Marigold sent a withering look in my direction as she emerged on the roof terrace with the *pantzarosalata*. As I jumped up to relieve Marigold of the beetroot salad she hissed "Really Victor, need you be quite so obvious? Putting yourself next to the only unattached woman?"

"Are you insane, the blasted woman is a nightmare," I hissed back, appalled that Marigold could suppose for even one moment that I had deliberately engineered things to sit next to Sherry. I wondered if that dratted woman Despina was back in town, spreading her vicious brand of gossip in the village shop.

Inane small talk was the order of the day during the salad course. Marigold still smarting from the dress code dig led the chat about how all the latest fashions were available to ex-pats now that Marks and Spencer had opened a branch in town. Once the plates were clear I suggested Marigold put them into the dumbwaiter and I would send them down to the kitchen. The overgrown wisteria blocked our guests' direct view of Marigold piling the plates into the receptacle so they remained clueless that the dumbwaiter was actually nothing more than a bucket tied to a rope.

"You have a dumbwaiter; I wish I'd thought to tell the builders to fix one in my house," Sherry said enviously. Her tone dismissed the builders as of no consequence and I wondered if she'd failed to make the family connection between Barry and the Bucket household. Some of the Brits had an unfortunate tendency to look down on the hired help.

"But you don't have a roof terrace," I pointed out.

"But a dumbwaiter would still be an asset. I wonder why that English builder didn't suggest one when I showed him my mood board for my dining arrangements."

Rolling her eyes Marigold volunteered "well ours is a DIY job, let's just hope that it doesn't follow the usual pattern of Victor's handiwork."

Chapter 16

Let them Eat Soup

By the time I had lugged the tureen of soup up from the kitchen, uncertain if my improvised dumbwaiter could bear the weight, the wine had loosened everyone up, everyone apart from Lester that is. Sniffing his wine suspiciously as though his glass had accidentally been filled with vinegar instead of Lidl's finest, the cowed shoplifter sat in meek silence feigning an interest as Norman droned on about traffic cones. Apart from his incessant twitch Lester was unrecognisable as the opinionated and bullying twerp from the previous evening.

"Such delicious soup, Marigold," Doreen praised. "It reminds me of the traditional Greek fish soup we had on the coast recently."

"Actually it is French bouillabaisse," Marigold fibbed, determined to keep up the pretence of serving foreign fare in keeping with the group ethos of cooking up exotic food from a medley of different countries.

"I thought that had mussels in it," Doreen said.

"I had to improvise with the recipe, have you tried getting fresh mussels round here?" Marigold asked. "I got the fresh fish from Thomas when he came round with the fish van, but the only mussels I've come across are frozen ones in Lidl."

"How dreadful to be so limited in choice that you are reduced to shopping in such a common supermarket," Anne Trout opined, slurring her words as she threw out the 'common' slur, reminding me that she'd been well into a bottle of wine when she was supposed to be babysitting.

"It's very reasonably priced compared to the village store and it's not exactly as though we have a handy Tesco on the doorstep," Marigold snapped, her hackles rising at such a blatant display of snobbery.

"You don't appear to have any problem sinking Lidl wine," I added.

Completely ignoring my sarcastic, yet astute observation, Anne Trout continued to spout her snobbish nonsense. "I don't know how you possibly manage without a Waitrose in the village. Lester is very fussy about where I buy our perishables."

"But not so particular where he shoplifts them from," I muttered under my breath. Even though Marigold didn't catch what I said her withering look warned me to play nice so I deftly changed the subject, introducing a note of humour.

"My gardener chanced upon a tortoise the other evening. There was a bit of a language faux pas and I got the wrong end of the stick and thought he intended to turn it into soup," I announced to the table. My diverting anecdote was met with horrified stares of disbelief rather than the amusement I had anticipated.

"The gardener is Albanian," Marigold added hastily, as though that explained things. Her comment reminded me of Basil Fawlty's running gag, 'Please excuse him, he's from Barcelona,' but I appeared to be the only one to draw a parallel between Guzim and Manuel.

"I really must get one of those," Sherry piped up. Her noticeable failure to expound the point left it up in the air if she wanted to acquire a gardener or an Albanian, but nevertheless I made a mental note to watch out for any underhand attempts to poach Guzim. I certainly had no appetite for mucking the chickens out myself.

"I was rather hoping you could keep an eye on the baby tomorrow," Anne Trout said to Marigold. "I can't believe the way Cynthia has let herself go since living out here. I want to take her up to the nearest town and sort her out with some decent clothes; she is quite clueless without my guidance. She came home in the most shapeless polo shirt today, she looked such a fright. I've a terrible feeling it was made out of polyester, can you imagine anything more dreadful?"

"Actually it's modacrylic," I said.

"I beg your pardon," the Trout woman spluttered, slopping some wine in her soup. It was clear that even half-cut she didn't appreciate being contradicted.

BUCKET TO GREECE (VOL. 6)

"Cynthia's polo shirt, it's made from modacrylic, it's a flame resistant acrylic..."

"I say old chap, I never had you down as an expert on women's clothing," Milton guffawed.

"It's part of the repping uniform, I have an identical one. Neither of us wear them willingly, it's company policy that we spend the day sweating in non-breathable fabric," I explained.

"At least it's an improvement on that ghastly orange uniform," Marigold reminded me.

"Hopefully there will be a shop that sells decent tummy control underwear; Cynthia has developed a noticeable belly lately," Anne Trout continued.

"For heaven's sake, she's only just had a baby," Marigold pointed out, her exasperation beginning to show.

"That's hardly an excuse to give up bothering with one's appearance," Anne Trout responded.

"Cynthia always keeps her hair nice and glossy," I said, earning a withering look from Anne Trout. "Anyway you can't whisk Cynthia off to the shops tomorrow; they don't open on Sundays."

"Another reason why I can't imagine what

possessed Cynthia to settle down in the back of beyond instead of in Cheshire," Anne Trout said, continuing to talk her daughter down.

"I rather think meeting the man of her dreams had something to do with that," I stated.

Anne Trout stared at me blankly as if clueless what I was on about. "Barry," I explained.

"Oh yes Barry, I did warn Cynthia not to settle for the first man to come along and take an interest in her. It was very careless of Cynthia to go and get herself pregnant out here."

"It wasn't a shotgun wedding if that's what you're implying," I objected.

"Nevertheless there's surely nothing stopping them from moving back to England now, it would be so much more convenient for us if Cynthia lived nearby, but of course the selfish girl is only thinking of herself as usual. Perhaps you could have a word with your brother Marigold, and persuade him to return to England, I'm sure he'd be able to get a much better job over there. Lester is quite influential in insurance, a much more suitable career for our son-in-law rather than manual labouring," Anne Trout pressed, clueless Marigold would not take kindly to her darling brother being disparaged.

"Barry sold a perfectly good business back

in England to make the move and invest in a partnership with Vangelis. He's very happy working on house renovations and there's a lot of skill involved. He certainly doesn't need to rely on nepotism to get a job," Marigold said coldly while firing daggers at the troublemaking Trout woman.

"Barry sold a business in England. Surely you don't mean that he has a bit of money?" Anne Trout blurted.

"How do you think he managed to buy a house for cash?"

"I say, are we onto property prices already? The subject doesn't usually crop up till the pudding course," Milton interrupted, no doubt hoping to steer the conversation at his end of the table away from the mind-numbing subject of traffic cones.

The collective silence around the table was only broken when Sherry gleefully announced "I've been drawing up a list of group activities us ex-pats should throw ourselves into."

"We prefer to think of ourselves as European citizens with Greek residency, rather than ex-pats," Marigold said, adopting a haughty tone as she repeated an oft used phrase of mine. Coming out of my wife's mouth the words amazed me; whenever I said the exact same thing she usually accused me of sounding pompous. Catching Marigold and Doreen exchanging an eye-roll I surmised that the two women felt their noses were being pushed out of joint by the new-comer Sherry: after all Marigold and Doreen had always been the ones to lead the way in organising any ex-pat activities, from group dinner parties to Greek dancing classes, and it probably didn't help that Sherry was not only unattached but appeared to be a tad younger than them.

Oblivious to the simmering resentment she was stirring, Sherry carried on in her gung-ho, jolly-hockey-sticks manner. "I'm just brimming with ideas for fun group activities. I was thinking we should start a sewing circle and a book club."

"I'm already in the local sewing circle," Marigold said, reminding the others of how the Greek ladies had attempted to salvage Cynthia's cat mangled bridal veil.

"And I'm not much of a reader so I wouldn't really be interested in a book club," Norman added. "Now if you were thinking of a club for avid traffic cone spotters I'd be all in."

"Victor's the reader round here, always got

his nose stuck in some impenetrable old tome about hygiene or ancient Greece," Milton piped up.

"I was thinking of reading matter along more popular lines," Sherry pouted.

"I just make do with the latest airport bestsellers that the tourists leave in the book swaps down on the coast," Doreen said.

"I've quite an interest in erotica." Whilst Marigold and I attempted to stifle our laughter at Milton's remark, the others simply stared at him aghast as though he'd admitted to loitering in the streets wearing a flasher mac.

"We could organise English language classes for the Greek children in the village, give something back to the community and all that," Sherry bulldozed on, determined to organise us all.

"It may have escaped your notice but there aren't actually any children in the village apart from Nikoleta and Anastasia, and they are both a tad young for lessons yet," I pointed out.

"I think you're mistaken. I saw a young teen in the village shop," Sherry argued.

"Thalia doesn't live here; she's staying with her Aunt Tina for a couple of weeks. Anyway she received an excellent score in the Cambridge

English language proficiency examination," I said, proud that I'd been able to give the teen a few pointers on correct English usage.

"Well what about a choir then, I'm sure that we would all enjoy a jolly nice sing-along," Sherry continued.

"I'm tone deaf old girl," Milton stated.

"And according to my wife I sound like a cat that's been trod on," I protested.

"That's only when you let loose with your opera in the shower dear, you're getting quite a name for your catchy renditions of the latest Eurovision chart busters," Marigold laughed.

"There's endless options, am-dram, a knitting circle...an art group, doesn't anyone fancy painting watercolours or throwing some pots?" Sherry continued desperately. "I was rather hoping for a bit more enthusiasm."

"Perhaps you could drum up some interest amongst the local Greeks," I suggested, thinking our mad neighbour Kyria Maria would most likely take to throwing pots with a vengeance, but not in the way Sherry intended.

"I'd be up for an art group old girl," Milton piped up. Sherry flashed her horsey dentures in relief that someone was finally demonstrating enthusiasm for her ideas. "I don't mind posing for life drawing classes."

The relief drained instantly from Sherry's face, her expressive features depicting disgust as she no doubt imagined Milton casting aside the dirty raincoat she'd imagined him in after his erotica remark. I was forming the impression that Sherry was a tad prudish.

"Milton's just pulling your leg Sherry, do ignore him," Edna said, sending a withering look her husband's way.

"If you're keen on something to do you could always find a job," I suggested.

"Oh I wouldn't know where to start, I've never worked. I'm not qualified in anything and I flunked all my O levels," Sherry replied. "Henry never wanted me to get a job, he preferred me to spend my time on the charity circuit."

I was beginning to form a mental image of Sherry's former life as a lady who lunched. I could imagine her throwing herself into the sort of charitable fundraisers where the organisers patted themselves on the back for spending a fortune to barely raise enough to donate a tin of cat food to their favourite pet cause.

Ironically it seemed that Edna could read my train of thought, suggesting to Sherry, "You could help me take care of the local strays, now that is a good cause. Although Milton and I have adopted about twenty ferals the stray cat population does keep on breeding."

"I expect that's because Cynthia refuses to have that vile mutant cat of hers neutered, it's forever off on one of its raping sprees," I said. It hadn't escaped my notice that the growing population of ferals included many mini-replicas of the repugnant looking creature with the distinctive stripe. I was greatly relieved that Pickles only took after its feline father in looks, rather than inheriting its tendency to go sniffing after any random four legged-creatures.

"Dratted thing will mate with anything. Always on the prowl, our cats are terrified of it," Milton said.

"Well whatever their origins they certainly keep multiplying," Edna said. "I would really appreciate a hand feeding them…"

"This village appears overrun with the nasty creatures, they play havoc with my allergies. If do-gooders weren't so irresponsible as to feed them it would surely lead to a natural cull," Anne Trout said contemptuously. Her shockingly callous remark earned her withering looks from around the table of fawning cat owners.

"Edna would rather go hungry herself than see the local strays suffer," Milton declared, breaking the aggrieved silence.

"I'm thinking of starting a cat feeding station. If we arrange a collection point by the public bins people can deposit their leftovers there," Edna said.

"Oh that certainly sounds like a good cause we can all get behind," Sherry enthused.

"Have you lost your mind? It's an absolutely terrible idea to leave leftovers out by the bins," I objected. "It is an insanitary practice that will only encourage all manner of filthy vermin. I must put my foot down most strongly."

"Ah, does that mean you managed to get your foot in the door at the *Dimarcheio* with your bin sanitation ideas, old chap?" Milton asked.

"The new mayor is very receptive to my suggestions," I said. Even though I was yet to be appointed to any official sanitation position I had managed to bend the mayor's ear talking rubbish. "Perhaps you could put the collection point somewhere else, perhaps in Sherry's courtyard since she's so keen to get involved. After all her house is tucked away in an out-of-the way spot."

My suggestion earned me a beam of approval

from my wife.

"I'll save any leftover bouillabaisse for you to take home Sherry, you may as well start feeding the strays tonight as you're so keen," Marigold offered.

"Surely cats don't eat soup," Sherry protested, not so keen after all.

Sensing Sherry's reluctance to welcome the stray cat population of Meli into her courtyard Marigold insisted "Why ever not? Let them eat soup, I say."

"But won't you want the leftovers for your own lovely pedigrees?" Sherry said, trying to squirm out of being bamboozled.

"Oh no, Clawsome and Catastrophe prefer tinned cat food so you won't be depriving them," Marigold assured her. "Now who's for a nice slice of chocolate bundt cake, Victor found a most amusing little recipe for it? Even though I think it's technically German it has a Greek twist as I made it with local olive oil."

"The oil needed slurrying with a rod," I quipped. Since my little joke fell completely flat I hid my embarrassment by gathering up the soup bowls. Whilst I collected the dirty dishes and piled them into the bucket Marigold rushed down to the kitchen ready to retrieve the crockery and replace it with the chocolate bundt.

Chapter 17

Victor Loses his Temper

Once I'd yanked the cake aloft Marigold called up for me to send the dumbwaiter down again since she'd forgotten to add the cream. As I hoisted the cream upwards the rope went suddenly slack as the bucket came loose from its knot and hurtled towards the pavement below, an enormous clatter signalling the metal bucket smashing into the paving stones. The din reverberated in the silence of the village, setting all the local dogs off in a cacophony of outraged barking.

BUCKET TO GREECE (VOL. 6)

Leaning over the railings I watched in disbelief, spotting the tail end of Pickles as the frisky cat hurled itself out of the kitchen window. Landing in a puddle of cream Pickles immediately started to lick the pavement, demonstrating a complete lack of concern for any random muck in the creamy treat. Really, I wondered why I bothered scouring the cat feeding bowls when our pets were quite indiscriminate in lapping their food from contaminated pavements.

Returning to the roof terrace Marigold pragmatically announced, "It will be much better for our waistlines to eat the bundt without cream."

Marigold was slicing the cake when I heard someone calling my name from the street. Leaning over the railings I spotted Spiros shooing off a dozen strays fighting over the cream. Spiros retrieved my runaway bucket from the middle of the street where it presented a traffic hazard and plonked it safely down on the pavement.

"Up here, Spiro, do come up and join us," I shouted down. I was pleased to see my good friend, finding his company much more entertaining than that of anyone at our dismal ex-pat gathering.

Clearly surprised to find a group of British

ex-pats in attendance Spiros apologised for dropping in spontaneously.

"Nonsense, come and join us," Marigold invited. "We've a spare seat since Felix didn't turn up. Can I tempt you with some bouillabaisse Spiro?"

"*Ti?*" Spiros asked.

"*Psarosoupa*," I said. Since I doubted anyone at the table would be able to translate the Greek word for fish soup, Marigold's attempts to pass off my Greek recipe as French would not be exposed. Noticing that Sherry's attention perked up with Spiros' arrival I discreetly hissed in his ear that it may be in his best interest to play dumb and mindlessly repeat 'I don't understand' should he become the object of her interest.

"I have no the interest in the single woman, the Sampaguita return on next the Thursday. I drive to the Athens airport to meet her," Spiros said. Since Spiros had been pining for Sampaguita he had taken less than his usual interest in village affairs and had not yet run into Sherry. "I come to bring the Marigold the gift."

"Oh Spiro, how kind, I love *loukoumi*," Marigold simpered when Spiros handed her a box of rose scented Turkish delight.

BUCKET TO GREECE (VOL. 6)

"It is the small thank you for talking to the Sampaguita; before you telephone she would not to admit to me she have overhear the nasty whisper. It upset her to hear the people gossip she stay in the Meli to catch the rich husband," Spiros said. "It make her feel the shame, on top of the guilt she feel about the dead uncle."

"I think it's wonderful that Sampaguita is returning soon, you make such a lovely couple," Marigold cooed.

With Marigold chatting to Spiros, Doreen took the opportunity to zoom in on me, asking how work was going. I told her I'd spent the day ferrying a coachload of tourists to Vathia and my next repping excursion would be the lazy day cruise.

"I think you could twist my arm for a day out on a cruise. I'll tell Cynthia to wangle a couple of free tickets for me and Lester," Anne Trout interrupted. "What day is it?"

"Tuesday, but Cynthia is working in the office and I think she's rather relying on you to babysit until Sampaguita gets back to Greece," I said rather curtly, irritated by the Trout woman's presumption in expecting a free day out on my watch. I could well imagine she would litter the customer satisfaction survey with critical comments even if she did get a freebie.

"Surely Cynthia can find someone else to watch the baby for the day," Anne Trout said. Poking Marigold in the arm she rudely interrupted her conversation with Spiros. "Can you look after the baby on Tuesday? Your husband has invited Lester and me to go on the lazy day cruise with him."

Marigold appeared rather taken back. "As much as I love spending time with Anastasia, I do have plans for Tuesday..."

"Surely you can change them...I can't imagine you have anything exciting on that you can't postpone, the social life in these parts strikes me as exceedingly dull," Anne Trout said, the odd inebriated hiccup mixed in with her words.

"I would never dream of letting the local ladies down by missing the meeting to beautify the graveyard..." Marigold began.

"Whether my wife's plans are exciting or not is rather beside the point," I interrupted, struggling to keep control of my temper in the face of Anne Trout's appalling sense of entitlement. An image of Cynthia's weary downtrodden face flashed before me and I recalled her anguished desperation when she returned home to discover no sign of the baby; it struck me that her mother deserved a verbal lashing.

"I thought the whole reason you were here was to give Cynthia a hand with the baby, not to palm your granddaughter off on my wife at every opportunity."

"Today was the first time I asked Marigold to give me a hand looking after Anastasia."

"Today was the first time that Cynthia entrusted you to babysit. You didn't ask Marigold to give you a hand, you dumped the baby on her for the day and then had the brass neck to tell Cynthia you were worn out from babysitting," I retorted.

"Well really, I don't see what business of yours it is…"

"It is my business: you tried to make a mug of my wife and no one gets away with that. You reduce poor Cynthia to a bag of nerves with your constant criticism and ever since you arrived in Meli you have done nothing but create extra work for her."

"What nonsense," Anne Trout protested.

"Is it nonsense that you have expected Cynthia to wait on you hand and foot? You haven't lifted a finger to help her with the cooking, just simply barked orders. I heard you complain that she didn't leave you any lunch today; what's that all about? Too bone idle to make a sandwich? You even insisted on taking over Cynthia and Barry's bedroom."

"Well we are guests. Cynthia couldn't possibly expect us to rough it in that undecorated spare bedroom they were using as a storage tip."

"You didn't give them any choice in the matter, you took over. It's a wonder Barry hasn't moved out, I don't know how he puts up with your insufferable ways, not to mention your husband's antics."

"How dare you speak to me like that," Anne Trout hiccupped. "Lester, are you going to allow him to speak to me in that way?"

"I say…" Lester began to say, his eye twitching manically. Catching my eye he realised I wouldn't hesitate to expose his shop lifting antics if he dared to pipe up.

"I've had enough of your insults," Anne Trout shouted, apparently more used to dishing them out than receiving them. "Come on Lester, we're leaving."

"Make sure you don't wake the baby when you roll back in," I spat as the Trouts flounced off, clinging woozily to the shaky balustrade lining the hazardous stone stairs.

"Victor, what on earth got into you?" Marigold asked, clearly awed by my performance. Looking around the table I realised our remaining guests were sitting all agog, perhaps wondering what I'd do for an encore. A wave of shame washed over me; my little outburst was completely out of character. About to apologise for my impetuous behaviour I was rather taken aback when Marigold added, "I have to say you were rather magnificent Victor."

"So manly," Doreen said.

"Never could abide the sort who don't love cats, what. Something amiss with the way their brains are wired," Milton added.

Everyone bonded together in general agreement that the Trouts were insufferable. The way in which Anne had spoken about Barry and Cynthia was nothing less than contemptible and had not gone unnoticed. No one could understand why the Trouts weren't rallying round to help care for their adorable grandbaby. Glad to be rid of the toxic guests we shared a nightcap of Metaxa companionably in the peace of the evening, the musky scent of the wisteria mixed with the lingering smell of Spiros' formaldehyde washing over us in the light breeze.

"Oh gosh, there appears to be some kind of creature in your garden, I can hear something crashing around down there. It sounds enormous," Sherry squealed. "You don't suppose it's one of those terrifying wild boars?"

"There's definitely something prowling down there, perhaps we should go and investigate," Marigold said, her words a natural cue for our guests to drain their Metaxa and announce their departure.

As we trooped down to the garden en-masse Marigold veered off into the house, saying "Victor, I'm just going to turn on the outside light, it may disturb whatever is down there."

"I say, do be careful old chap, you can't fight off a wild boar without a weapon," Milton advised as we reached the garden. The noise was emanating from the grape arbor; I tentatively approached, the others huddling fearfully in my wake. Grabbing a sweeping brush as a likely weapon I wielded it as though I meant business.

"Oh this is so scary, do you suppose that wild boars eat people?" Shelley yelped, the others shushing her.

The grape arbor was suddenly flooded with light as Marigold hit the upstairs switch. I gasped in shock, confronted by an utterly gruesome sight. I would have much preferred to have encountered a wild boar on the loose rather than be surprised by Guzim soaking himself in my new pristinely scrubbed bathtub.

The shameless Albanian shed dweller was floating up to his neck in bubbles, clutching my prized esoteric backscratcher which I presumed he intended to use to scrub off his grime. I was taken aback, wondering how Guzim had managed to fill the bath since my hosepipe was safely locked away out of his reach in the downstairs storage and his own bit of pipe wouldn't stretch from his shed. Guzim dropped the backscratcher; it landed with a clatter on top of the metal bucket that had recently served as my dumbwaiter. By a process of deduction I surmised that Guzim must have claimed the runaway bucket from the street and used it to fill the tub, helping himself to a generous measure of the expensive coconut scented bubble bath I had treated myself to in anticipation of a long outdoor soak.

"Guzim, *fyge apo ekei tora,*" I yelled. Guzim looked horrified to be caught out, his eyes darting around nervously like a trapped animal. Clearly he hadn't expected to find his nocturnal bathing scrutinised by a gawping party of dumbstruck ex-pats.

"No Victor, don't tell him to get out," Marigold shouted, peering down from above. "There are ladies present. I'll never live it down if Guzim flashes them at my dinner party."

Unable to understand Marigold's cry of protest Guzim stirred in the water, pulling himself upright as I repeated my demand that he get out of the bath. Obviously cowed by my stern tone Guzim made a move to stand up just as Sherry shrieked "No, I can't cope with the sight of a naked man," making no attempt to avert her eyes.

"Get a grip," Edna told her. "All those bubbles will cover his bits."

The dinner party guests all exhaled in relief when Guzim stepped out of the bath, revealing nothing more than his revolting habit of bathing in his underpants.

Chapter 18

Buttering Up with Bacon

Having carefully prepared some grammatically correct Greek spiel in order to give Guzim a translated piece of my mind, I was rather put out to discover no sign of the Albanian shed dweller lurking outdoors the next morning. The only evidence of his nocturnal activities was a grimy tidemark ringing the outside bathtub and a pair of damp underpants flapping on the washing line.

Taking a turn around the garden I surveyed the vegetable patch with a sense of pride. My hard work had paid off, making us almost self-sufficient in vegetables, with plenty to spare to spare for our neighbours. My irritation with Guzim lessened when I realised the vegetable patch wouldn't be a patch of its bountiful self without his tireless help. Noticing that the red peppers were beginning to ripen nicely I imagined charring them under the grill to release their distinct sweetness; roasted red pepper soup with a garnish of fresh basil is one of my favourite summer dishes.

We certainly had a glut of green peppers, far more than we had use for. Thinking I would share the bounty amongst the villagers later, I picked a handful for Kyria Maria and popped them into the bucket on top of the garden wall. The bucket served as a mutual bartering receptacle between our two houses. Maria was always grateful to receive my veggies; in return she often added all manner of odds and sods to the bucket when she returned the gesture. Just two days ago I had left her some plump purple aubergines, only to return later to find she had left me some crocheted antimacassars. Whilst I had been confused by this offering at least it increased my Greek vocabulary; checking my dictionary I learnt that the protective squares are conveniently called *antimacassars* in Greek. I was no longer surprised to discover some dregs in an almost empty plastic bottle of wine or some carefully wrapped up leftovers which I presumed she intended for the cats. I suspected Maria sometimes used the bucket as a convenient method of disposing of her rubbish rather than walking to the bins. However I never complained about carting her rubbish away along with our own since it was a marked improvement on the days when she used to burn her refuse in the garden and practically suffocate us with the stench of burning plastic.

Captain Vasos had boasted he would catch me a fresh fish on the next lazy day cruise. Assuming he would be sober enough to remember his promise, a bit of a leap admittedly, I envisaged pan frying the catch and serving it with garden fresh new potatoes and steamed home grown green beans. Unfortunately my garden remained bereft of the type of new potatoes I was craving; delicious small Jerseys cooked in their skins and smothered in butter.

I had sought the advice of the local Greeks regarding the kind of seed potatoes I needed to plant in order to grow a potato crop similar to Jerseys, but my attempt to make them understand quite what I was after fell spectacularly flat. Panos had simply loaded me up with an enormous sack of oversized potatoes from his own garden, scratching his head and looking flummoxed as he pointed to their *dermata*, or skins. Whilst they were undoubtedly excellent potatoes of the finest quality, alas they bore no resemblance to the dainty Jerseys I had in mind. I fared little better with Nikos when I shared my new potato frustration with him.

"The Dina always to peel the potato, we not to eat the dirty skin," Nikos chortled, immediately telling his wife that I had some strange foreign habit of eating potato skins. When I left the taverna later that night Dina pressed a paper bag full of potato peelings on me, worriedly asking if my finances were so dire that I needed a few shifts in the taverna kitchen. Obviously word of my strange foreign predilection for eating potato skins must have spread like wildfire through the village: in recent days the bucket on the garden wall had been filled with Kyria Maria's old scrapings.

Wandering over to the chicken run to check on my flock I noticed the ground had been neatly raked and was clean of droppings; I presumed that Guzim had done an early muck run to avoid a stern tongue-lashing. Raki, the chicken with the gammy leg, grubbed around in the dirt next to Frappé, the newly resident tortoise. Frappé had somehow managed to get its head stuck between the wire netting whilst chomping on a wild sage bush. I carefully released it from the trap, recoiling from the repugnant touch of its dry and wrinkled scaly skin, the speed at which its block-shaped head darted back into its shell surprising me.

It occurred to me that I had been terribly remiss in not considering the potential risks of penning the tortoise in with our livestock since tortoises are well known carriers of salmonella germs; my casual oversight meant we could well end up with infected eggs. I imagined Guzim doing a roaring trade flogging salmonella infected droppings to gullible ex-pats down on the coast, picturing them spreading it liberally on their vegetable patches. Not only would it be terribly embarrassing if any subsequent outbreak of food poisoning was traced back to the chicken run of a retired public health inspector, but it would ruin my credibility as the local authority on germs.

I made a hasty decision based on nothing more than a suspicion that the tortoise was a ticking time bomb of unexploded, potentially lethal bacteria; there was nothing else for it, the tortoise would have to go. Since Guzim appeared unnaturally fond of the new arrival I imagined he may well remark upon its sudden disappearance; I would need to concoct a likely story that conveniently omitted any reference to salmonella. I would surely appear more empathetic if I was to declare I had returned the noble creature to its natural habitat and released it to the wild.

I reflected that no matter how exalted the tortoise may be in the local animal hierarchy it didn't lessen my compelling need to scour my hands after touching the potentially germ ridden creature, a need that struck me as a higher priority than scoping out a suitable olive grove to dump the tortoise in. Presuming that since it was Sunday Kyria Maria would be safely ensconced in church, I took the liberty of scaling the garden wall and gently depositing the tortoise in her garden. No doubt she would be delighted to discover it had randomly wandered in; she may even find it an excellent companion as long as it kept its distance from the chicory plants so beloved by Papas Andreas.

Back indoors I applied a generous measure

of hand sanitiser and reflected that Guzim was not the only early riser. Marigold had been up with the lark, treating me to the unheard of luxury of coffee in bed before disappearing to the shop, promising to cook me a special breakfast on her return. My wife's behaviour was so out of character that it set of my radar detector and made me question her motives; I pondered what she could be after now. No doubt she would begin to drop some rather unsubtle hints about a swanky mini-break at some shockingly overpriced luxury hotel in Athens. I decided that no matter how much it would pain me to flash the credit card, I would play along; after all I would soon have some buttering up of my own to do if I expected Marigold to put up with my plan of installing Violet Burke in our downstairs storage.

"The shop is heaving this morning, it took an age to get served," Marigold announced on her return, flashing a packet of bacon under my nose and treating me to an unexpected kiss.

"I expect the locals were stocking up on cigarettes before church, you know how those services drag on," I said. It always amused me to spot supposedly devout church goers popping out mid-sermon for a crafty cigarette break.

"You're probably right. I felt quite guilty sneaking by Papas Andreas, all done up in his Sunday best, but he knows I'm not of the orthodox persuasion. I think our attending the midnight *Pascha* service may have got his hopes up that we would turn into church going regulars. Now you just relax darling, I'm doing bacon sandwiches for breakfast."

Ever since we'd committed to a healthier Greek diet, fried bacon had been on Marigold's list of banned goodies. It often struck me as a tad hypocritical that my wife was happy to stuff her face with sugary Greek confections such as *halva* and *bougatsa*, but put her foot down when it came to the good old British classic of a bacon butty. Unfortunately as Marigold can detect the illicit smell of fried bacon at fifty paces I can't even get away with a spot of surreptitious frying when she's out.

The prospect of bacon made me appreciate that the threat of being arrested for illegal Sunday trading was no deterrent to Tina opening the shop. Against the soothing background sound of sizzling bacon I once again began to mentally question my wife's aberrant behaviour. Whilst coffee in bed had struck me as a none-too-subtle bribe for a mini-break, Marigold had definitely upped the stakes with the bacon: perish the thought that she was buttering up me for a foreign cruise or that she was back to hankering after a swimming pool.

"This is a real treat Marigold," I said, hoping she would divulge her ulterior motives rather than keep me guessing.

"You deserve it darling," she replied, tantalising my taste buds by spreading lashings of Colman's English mustard on the toasted bread. "The way you stood up for me at the ex-pat dinner party made me realise just how lucky I am to have such a wonderful husband. I should have listened when you warned me that Cynthia's mother was a malicious woman, but I didn't see it until last night. I couldn't believe the way she looked down on Meli and denigrated Barry, and I think it was more than just the wine talking."

"Starving the cats was a gem. I warned you she was pure poison," I gloated. "And I'm afraid that's not all; I didn't want to upset you by saying anything just before dinner but the reason I dashed to the shop yesterday was because Tina called in a terrible flap. She caught Lester shoplifting and thought it would be more expedient if I dealt with the matter rather than calling the police."

"Oh my, that's awful, what on earth would possess him to stoop so low? And to think Anne Trout looked down on us...oh goodness, we gave him house room, we'd better make sure nothing is missing."

"I don't think he'd dare pilfer from us after he was caught red-handed in the shop, he seemed pretty desperate that Barry and I wouldn't blab to Anne or Cynthia," I said.

"Yes, best if the two of you keep schtum, Cynthia has enough on her plate without discovering her father is nothing but a petty thief," Marigold sighed. "Anyway, apart from the ghastly Trouts and that terribly embarrassing scene with Guzim, the dinner party seemed to go off remarkably well."

Nodding in agreement I was heartened that my wife made no reference to my bungled DIY job with the improvised dumbwaiter.

"I don't think anyone suspected your bouillabaisse wasn't authentic and the chocolate bundt turned out a treat," I said as Marigold passed me a bacon sandwich. Biting into the hot toasted bread I savoured the crisp texture of the bacon and the sharp hit of mustard, bacon fat dripping onto my fingers and turning them greasy. Tempted though I was to lick them clean I didn't fancy ruining the delicious taste of bacon by getting a mouthful of hand sanitiser; besides it was much too early in the day for alcohol.

"Did I mention that Sherry was in the shop earlier?" Marigold said, chasing the last few toast crumbs round her plate. "She was carrying on as though I was her new best chum, insisting on inviting us round for Sunday lunch."

"Tell me you didn't accept," I groaned.

"Of course not, I had more than enough of Sherry's bombastic enthusiasm last night, it was quite exhausting. I came up with a rather lame excuse, saying we had plans to go out and crossing my fingers she wouldn't suggest joining us... we might have to pretend we aren't at home if she comes checking up."

I groaned at the thought, recalling the many occasions we had been forced to pretend we weren't in to avoid Harold and Joan bombarding us with constant invitations to their ghastly pool parties. The last thing we needed was another over-enthusiastic British neighbour desperate to latch on.

"There's a simple remedy to that," I said. "We won't be at home as I'm going to whisk you off to a lovely secluded cove where we can enjoy a nice dip."

"Oh Victor, that sounds perfect," Marigold trilled. She seemed genuinely delighted by my suggestion. If there had been an ulterior motive behind the bacon sandwiches she was yet to spring it on me. "Of course we can't always go out to avoid Sherry so we must think up a more practical way of dealing with the situation."

"You sound as though you have something in mind."

"Well it's obvious that the only reason she's so desperate to involve us all in group activities is because she's on her own. A spot of matchmaking could be the answer...all we have to do is fix her up with an available man."

"Hmm," I said noncommittally, recalling Marigold's last meddling attempt at matchmaking had not gone quite to plan. When her friend Geraldine was staying with us Marigold had invited a selection of eligible local bachelors to a dinner party, dangling them in front of her friend like a range of juicy morsels. Despite the choice selection of single men lined up for Geraldine, a most unsuitable candidate had caught her eye when the local cleric Papas Andreas, a man who had vowed to lead a celibate single life, arrived at the dinner party looking for his mother. There was an instant spark of passion between the Papas and Geraldine, a magnetic pull neither of them could resist, the unlikely pair soon sneaking around to engage in illicit assignations in the church.

When Geraldine returned to England the Papas had pressed me for English lessons so he could spice up the sweet nothings he drooled down the long distance telephone line. Of course it was obvious to anyone with a half a brain that their forbidden relationship could lead nowhere, a realisation that must have finally dawned on Geraldine when she recently took up with a science bod who spent his working day analysing bodily samples for sexually transmitted infections. She was yet to break the news to the esteemed cleric that she was walking out with a new fellow. The whole pathetic saga did not put Marigold's matchmaking in a good light, but nevertheless it didn't deter her from further meddling.

"Of course Spiros is practically spoken for now, but Dimitris and Panos are still available," Marigold mused.

"Sherry would eat Dimitris alive, you know he prefers a quiet life, and I can't help but notice that Panos is rather taken with my mother," I pointed out.

"Instead of being negative you could try wracking your brain to see if you can think of any suitable single men," Marigold chided.

"Well since Sherry clearly loves the sound of her own voice there's always Captain Vasos' mute sidekick Sami. I doubt any chap she takes up with would be able to get a word in," I suggested.

"There's no need to be sarcastic Victor...I know, we can invite Sherry to tag along to Apostolos' name day party..."

"I'm pretty sure that the local barber is married."

"Of course he is; his wife makes the most delicious *kataifi* for when all the ladies get together to beautify the cemetery...but there's sure to be a selection of unattached men at the party."

"I presume you realise Sherry's husband must have been considerably older than her," I said. Marigold raised an eyebrow so I expounded my theory. "Felix is at least a decade older than his step-mother..."

"Ah, I see where you're coming from; if she has a thing for older men that certainly makes things much easier as it widens the potential dating pool considerably…one can hardly move in Meli without tripping over elderly single men."

Hearing movement on the outside staircase I said, "It sounds as though we've got visitors; let's hope it's not Sherry."

We both exhaled in relief when Barry popped his head round the door, manoeuvring the pram into the kitchen.

"I say, is that bacon I can smell?"

Chapter 19

A Convenient Scapegoat

"Oh lovely, you've brought the baby round for a visit," Marigold gushed, immediately rushing over to pick up Anastasia and shower her with kisses. "You really need to get one of those strappy baby carriers rather than bumping the pram up the outside stairs."

"A baby carrier is a bit of a risk. Every old dear in the village swoops on the pram as it is; they'd be invading my personal space if the baby was strapped to my chest," Barry guffawed.

"Get away with you, you love the attention. You have every granny for miles wishing you were still single," Marigold laughed.

"Take a seat, you look done in," I invited, observing that even the bags below Barry's eyes had bags of their own. "I have to say you're looking a tad haggard this morning, did the baby keep you up?"

"She was sleeping like an angel until the Trouts woke her with their carryings on," Barry said, gratefully accepting a cup of strong coffee.

"If this is related to their bedroom activities I don't think you should say anymore in front of the baby, she's much too sweet and innocent to hear about such nasty things," Marigold quipped.

"I'd rather have put up with squeaking bedsprings than the Trouts drunken fight," Barry sighed, gulping his coffee. "They had an almighty row when they rolled back in from your dinner party. Luckily Cynthia bunged the ear plugs in before sleeping since it was my turn to get up with the baby, so she was spared the sound of their ugly fracas, but I had the misfortune to overhear everything."

V.D. BUCKET

"Anne certainly sank plenty of wine, even though it came from Lidl," I said, beginning to feel I'd rather overdone it a tad with a second bacon butty.

"Let me guess, Waitrose popped up as her sparkling brand of dinner party conversation," Barry said, acknowledging my nod of confirmation.

"She certainly gave Norman's traffic cones a run for their money," I noted.

"It was terribly inconsiderate of them to have a late night fight and wake Anastasia," Marigold said before cooing over the baby in a soppy voice, "Yes, wasn't it naughty of your granny and granddad to wake you up, they're so naughty, yes."

"What were they arguing about?" I asked.

"Well the usual meek and mild Lester who never stands up to his wife managed to grow a pair and berate her for the insufferable way she carried on at your dinner party. I can only imagine the sort of things she came out with," Barry confided, happy to spill the beans. "Lester accused Anne of being too sozzled to realise she had revealed how barbaric she was by suggesting to a bunch of dim witted cat lovers that the best way of dealing with the stray population was to let them starve."

"I did consider it very restrained of our guests not to lynch her when she came out with that," Marigold said.

"Lester told Anne he was thoroughly ashamed of the contemptible way she spoke about their daughter in public. From their screeching match I gather she must have aired her views about my shortcomings as her son-in-law too…"

"She's certainly not a fan. She went over the top with her carping criticisms and can you believe she suggested buying Cynthia tummy flattening underwear in front of a group of strangers, it was quite mortifying to hear," Marigold sighed.

"I don't think you'd have been her first pick as a son-in-law," I said to Barry. "Even so she let us know that she'd rather the pair of you decamped to Cheshire…"

"Where's the logic in that when she clearly can't stand me? Why would she want me in England?"

"I imagine so that Cynthia will be at her beck and call whilst she drips her poison about how unsuitable you are. Of course the Trout woman has plans to improve you by having

Lester use his influence to get you a job in insurance," I said.

"Oh spare me, can you imagine me in an office, I'd go stir crazy. I've never been happier since moving out here, that is until the Trouts landed on our doorstep," Barry said. "I still can't get over the way Lester ripped into his wife, even calling out her drinking. She usually uses him as a doormat and up until now he seemed quite content for her to wipe her feet all over him."

"Victor may have been responsible for that," Marigold suggested. "He rather lost his temper and gave your stuck-up mother-in-law a thorough dressing-down."

"Drat, I wish I'd been there to see you take her down a peg, *bravo* Victor. It sounds as though you may have had a hand in Lester's decision to leave."

"They are leaving…or just Lester?" Marigold queried, looking confused.

"Well there's the rub. Lester told Anne that after the way she'd carried on they had to pack up their suitcases and leave Meli. He insisted she left him with no choice as he'd never be able to hold his head up in the village again."

"Ah, now it all comes together. Lester is using

his wife as a convenient scapegoat in case word of his own petty thievery slips out. If he can persuade her to up and leave she won't get wind of him stuffing his pockets with purloined bars of chocolate," I said.

"I'd say you've hit the nail on the head there Victor. Lester certainly didn't have a problem with his wife's attitude until it became convenient to use it as an excuse to cover his own tracks," Barry agreed.

Raising my coffee cup in a celebratory toast I said, "Here's to you getting rid of your vile in-laws."

"I'm not quite counting my chickens yet; Anne pulled out her trump card, saying they couldn't possibly leave until Anastasia was baptised," Barry sighed.

"Can I tempt you with a bacon butty, Barry?" Marigold asked, passing me the baby. Anastasia took one look at me and broke into an adorable gummy smile, instantly melting my heart.

"'Fraid not, I'm fit to bursting already, the mother-in-law did me a full English before I came out," Barry said between wide yawns.

Catching Marigold and I exchanging quizzical glances Barry explained that the woman who claimed to be unable to lift a finger in a confusing Greek kitchen had apparently decided to turn over a new leaf, beginning by buttering up her husband and son-in-law with a cooked breakfast while Cynthia enjoyed a lie-in.

"So clearly a transparent manoeuvre to get on your good side, perhaps she thinks if she comes across as a reformed character she can hang around for a bit longer sunning herself in the Greek sunshine," Marigold scoffed.

"Having lowered everyone's defences with a superb fry-up Anne told Lester she was happy to head home as soon as they'd seen their granddaughter baptised. I'm afraid she managed to badger him into caving in and agreeing they should be at the christening."

"But you haven't even arranged anything yet," Marigold said. "Are you sure I can't tempt you with a bacon butty, Barry?"

"No really, thanks anyway. I only popped round to see if I can borrow Victor for a bit..."

"Well we're off for a swim shortly but I can spare him if you don't keep him away for too long," Marigold said.

"What have you got in mind?" I asked.

"I thought we could catch up with Papas Andreas when he finishes the morning service and see if we can pin him down to the earliest possible date for Anastasia's baptism...I might need you to translate if he starts spouting clerical Greek, my builder's lingo isn't really suitable for the ears of a man of God," Barry laughed.

"Oh, he strikes me as quite broadminded; I don't think the odd bit of colourful language would faze him. Still you can always count on my support," I said. "I just hope you don't have to bung him a brown envelope."

"Since neither of you fancy anymore bacon can you wheel the baby out to the balcony, I don't want to asphyxiate her with this," Marigold said, frantically shaking a can of air freshener, determined to eradicate all lingering aromas of the wonderful breakfast.

Chapter 20

Macaroni and Meatballs

Marigold claimed dibs on the baby whilst Barry and I headed off to waylay Papas Andreas. As we trooped down the stairs the sound of Marigold cooing over our baby niece drifted down, "Shall we go and have a look at the lovely chicks and the tortoise my precious darling, yes, lovely chicks." I felt a twinge of guilt that by dumping the tortoise in the neighbouring garden I had deprived Anastasia of her first glimpse of the slow moving reptile, but reasoned she was still too young to be able to differentiate between the shelled creature and the resident egg layers.

We bumped into Papas Andreas on our way to the church. After exchanging greetings Barry begged for a moment of his time. The Papas revealed he was off to visit his mother and insisted we accompany him. Despite living next door to Kyria Maria for almost two years, during which time she has barged into our home on countless occasions, I had not as yet been invited to cross the neighbouring threshold though I had been caught out scaling the garden wall several times.

Maria's house was much smaller than ours. The main door opened directly from the street and led into the sitting room, notable for its gloomy aspect. Just enough light filtered in through the hand-embroidered lace panels covering the small windows overlooking the street for me to see that the room was dominated by dark wooden furniture and religious icons, giving an impression of clutter. Before I had chance to take full stock of my surroundings Andreas ushered us through to the kitchen, pausing to say, "I must to warn you the Mama may not be the happy…"

"Oh, we really don't want to intrude," I protested.

"No, no, you not to intrude, but after the church the Mama complain,

how to say in the English..."

"That the service drags on too long," I suggested, giving voice to a common grievance I'd heard bandied around the village.

"No, not that," Andreas said, a puzzled frown marring his handsome features at the very idea he may drone on a tad. "Mama not to like the smoker walking the in and out..."

"Ah, I imagine she finds it a tad disrespectful..."

"No, she complain they disturb her when she sleep."

I kept my own counsel since it appeared the Papas did not draw the evident connection between his long-winded sermons and his mother falling asleep in church.

Entering the kitchen I was almost knocked out by the suffocating heat. There was no sign of Maria, but a pan of something simmering on the old fashioned cast iron wood-fuelled stove explained the stifling temperature. The table was set for two, the plastic tablecloth adorned with sunflowers adding a touch of cheer to the dated room that was in desperate need of a face lift.

BUCKET TO GREECE (VOL. 6)

"*Pou eisai Mama? Echoume episkeptes,*" Andreas called out, asking where his mother was and alerting her they had visitors.

"*Ston kipo,*" Maria called back from the garden. It was a relief to step outside to join her and escape the unnatural heat of the kitchen.

Maria was stooped over, her back towards us, her attention focused on something in the chicory plants. "*Koita,*" she called, turning round and gesturing for us to look, her voice quivering with excitement. Despite Andreas' heads up that his mother would not be in the best of tempers, Maria was grinning from ear to ear. "*Koita, mia helona,*" 'look, a tortoise.'

I had not seen Maria look so elated since she sank her wizened old body in Harold's swimming pool. Even though her discovery of Frappé in the garden was clearly a source of delight, I decided to play dumb and pretend to be surprised. With my cover story to maintain that I had returned Frappé to the wild I didn't want to blunder in by assuming Maria was overjoyed at the prospect of a new garden companion; it could yet turn out she was thrilled at the thought of free meat and planned to cook the creature up. Kyria Maria could be a tad temperamental; if the tortoise was going to turn up in a new recipe that made her sick she may well accuse me of trying to infect her with salmonella if I confessed to a prior knowledge of the slow intruder I had unceremoniously dumped in her garden.

"*Mou aresei poly i helona,*" Maria gushed, telling us she loved the tortoise very much. I had no idea she would be so taken with the creature, having never pegged Maria as an animal lover since she had the habit of chasing away any cats that got into her garden with a broomstick. Maria added that she had seen on the television that tortoises were good luck: "*Eida stin tileorasi oti i helona einai kali tychi.*"

"*Den akousa pote oti i helones itan tycheri Mama,*" Andreas said, telling her he had never heard that tortoises were lucky.

"*Nai nai, einai tycheroi stin Kina.*" Maria's argument that they were lucky in China was one we couldn't counter. Andreas wasn't buying it, politely proclaiming in English that it was superstitious nonsense, aware his mother wouldn't understand the foreign language putdown. I had to stifle my laughter when Maria added that if she kept the tortoise it meant she would be rich in her old age. Apparently, in Maria's mind, at the ripe old age of eighty-two she was still a youngster.

Bending down Maria scooped up the tortoise, cradling it like a baby and declaring it would be an excellent companion, though not quite as chatty as my mother who she said she was missing very much. Cuddling the tortoise Maria enquired about the health of Violet Burke, Marigold, Cynthia, and the baby, before insisting we stay for something to eat. Barry and I, both already stuffed full of bacon, protested we were fine, but Maria would not take no for an answer, determined to feed us up even though it was mid-way between breakfast and lunchtime and the Greeks weren't renowned for eating brunch. Knowing it would be impolite to refuse we girded ourselves for yet more food. Neither of us could work up an appetite so soon after such satisfying breakfasts.

We were just about to adjourn indoors for the unwanted meal when a familiar voice piped up from the other side of the garden wall: "Victor, *esy eisai*?" I recognised the guttural tones of Guzim asking if it was me. No sooner had I identified the voice than Guzim's head popped into view over the wall, a look of worried anguish plastered across his grimy features.

"*Leipei to Frappé, koitazo pantou,*" Guzim

practically sobbed as he told me that Frappé was missing and he had looked everywhere for it.

Clueless that the Frappé my gardener was referring to was a tortoise rather than an actual frothy coffee, Maria spat under her breath "*afto einai panta meta apo enan dorean kafe,*" meaning, 'that one is always after a free coffee.' My elderly neighbour had little tolerance for the Albanian shed dweller, having caught him showering under the outside hosepipe one time too many.

Spotting the tortoise Maria was still cradling, Guzim declared "*ekei, pos bike ston kipo tis grias?*" 'There it is, how did it get in the old woman's garden?'

Drawing myself up to my full height I assured Guzim that he was mistaken and he was looking at a completely different tortoise. Seemingly forgetting who pays his wages Guzim contradicted me, not only insisting the tortoise was definitely Frappé but that the old woman had stolen it.

"He to call my mother the thief," Papas Andreas said, seemingly unfazed by the accusation.

"He's got the wrong end of the stick," I said, completely befuddling Andreas. Although he had been keen to cram up on English sweet nothings to woo Geraldine, he had clearly not paid any attention to my lesson on common English idioms.

Turning my attention back to Guzim I told him he had lost his mind, insisting the tortoise bore not the slightest resemblance to the one that had previously resided in our chicken coop. To stress my point I addressed the tortoise directly by name: when the tortoise failed to respond I used this as evidence that Guzim had clearly muddled up his creatures. I could tell that the Albanian was not entirely convinced, but Kyria Maria settled the matter by dashing indoors and returning with a red indelible marker pen. Bending over the tortoise she scrawled the word MAPIA, the Greek spelling of her own name, on the shell. Triumphantly holding the tortoise aloft Maria said *"einai i helona mou kai to onomazo Mapia,"* meaning 'it is my tortoise and I name it Maria.'

Guzim stomped off, visibly disgruntled, so not much new there. Meanwhile the four of us retired to the kitchen, five of us if you count the newly named MAPIA whom Maria decreed would make a lovely house pet. I sighed in frustration: recalling Derek Little shutting his pet tortoise up in the family living room, I reflected that life had come full circle.

Maria busied herself setting an extra two places at the table before serving heaped platefuls of *macaronia* and *keftedes* from the simmering pan. Barry and I exchanged uneasy glances, unsure if our stomachs could take it. We were both familiar enough with Greek hospitality to know we had no choice but to force it down. Glancing surreptitiously at my watch I realised I would need to bolt the food since Marigold was expecting me to whisk her off to a romantic cove.

Even though I had little appetite, I had to admit that Kyria Maria cooked a mean meatball, the addition of spearmint and parsley a great success. Delicious though the *keftedes* were I struggled to finish the food. Maria continually chivvied me to "*troo, troo,*" leaving me with no alternative but to follow her demands that I eat. Her beady eyes monitored my every forkful, depriving me of the chance to discreetly pocket the odd meatball.

Forced to surreptitiously loosen my belt I hoped that Marigold wasn't expecting me to treat her to lunch out or I would surely explode. Maria topped up our glasses with white wine from a plastic bottle, seemingly unaware it was still only the middle of the morning. When I declined with the reasonable excuse that I needed to drive, Maria simply poured the wine into the bowl of water she'd put on the floor for the tortoise. Hopefully the alcohol would go some way towards obliterating any salmonella germs the creature harboured.

Maria rattled on so much about how adorable the baby was and how much she liked my mother, that Barry didn't have chance to raise the subject of the baptism. It was only when Maria sprang from the table, announcing she was popping upstairs to collect a gift she'd made for Anastasia, that Barry finally had the opportunity to ask the Papas about setting a date for the christening. Unfortunately for Barry it appeared that Andreas had simply been waiting for the opportunity to ask about Geraldine without his mother earwigging. Even though Maria does not understand English I imagined her ears pricking up if a strange woman's name rolled off her son's lips.

"Geraldine is very well," I told the Papas, wondering if I ought to break the news that she was walking out with a new chap. Although I felt it was not my place to be the bearer of bad news, I didn't approve of Geraldine stringing Andreas along. However since I had no way of knowing how the cleric would react if I was to spill the beans, I decided not to risk it. He may well end up too sad and maudlin to concentrate on finding a date in the church diary for the baptism. The thought of the affable cleric dripping tears on my shoulder did not fit in with my plans for the day.

Barry took the plunge, cutting the Papas off mid-sentence as he extolled Geraldine's virtues. Draining his glass Andreas shook his head as though shaking loose an image of the English woman. Getting down to business he ascertained that neither Barry nor Cynthia was of the orthodox persuasion, but appeared prepared to overlook this major hurdle since Barry had persuaded Vangelis and Athena to stand as godparents.

"The summer he is the very busy time in the calendar...you must to appreciate I have three the parishes to oversee," Andreas said before lapsing into Greek. *"To vaptisma, einai dyskolo, poly dyskolo. Isos den echo tipota mechri ton Septemvrio."*

Barry's face practically fell to the floor when the Papas told him it would be difficult and he may not have anything until September. There was clearly no way Barry could tolerate his intolerable in-laws living under his roof until then.

"*Alla einei epeigon,*" I interceded, stressing to the Papas it was urgent.

"*Epeigon.*" Repeating the word urgent Andreas cast an odd look in Barry's direction, perhaps pondering the likelihood that Barry had been overcome with religious fervour.

"Yes urgent, Barry has to suffer his in-laws living under his roof until the baptism," I explained.

"The shoplifter and the snob drunk? This is not the good, very not good," Andreas declared. I supposed it was not too surprising that gossip about Cynthia's parents must be rife in the village; it was impossible to keep anything private in such a small community. Leafing through his diary the Papas said "*Boro na kano to eponmeno Savvato.*"

"*To epomeno Savvato,*" Barry repeated.

"Yes, I can to do the baptism on the Saturday next," Andreas confirmed with a grin. "I know from the experience it is not the easy living with the difficult relative."

As if on cue the difficult relative Kyria Maria

returned to the kitchen, pressing a tissue wrapped parcel into my hands and announcing it was for the baby. I hoped that she wasn't coming down with a touch of Uncle Leo's affliction and confusing me with the new father, but she seemed as sharp as a tack. Papas Andreas announced he must be on his way, having promised to call in on some of his parishioners. Using his departure as a convenient cue to take our leave we followed him out. I couldn't help wondering if the leftover macaroni and meatballs would make an appearance in the garden wall bucket later.

Chapter 21

A Seat on the Board

"Can you imagine how Cynthia and Marigold are going to react when they hear they only have six days to prepare everything for the baptism?" Barry groaned as we left Maria's house.

"It's better than the alternative of you being stuck with the vile Trouts until September," I consoled him.

"I suppose I'd better break the news to Cynthia now. Can I twist your arm to come along and give me moral support? If Anne comes up with another excuse for not leaving immediately after the baptism you could take Lester aside and let him know his pilfering is already the talk of the village," Barry pleaded. It was clear he had no faith that Anne would abide by her promise to leave after the christening.

"Okay, but we need to be quick," I agreed as we walked towards the village square, the tempting blue of the sea in the distance reminding me that I'd promised to take my beloved for a swim. "Marigold is waiting for me to whisk her off to a romantic cove for a dip."

"She'll forgive you for a slight delay, you know she'll be in her element making a fuss of the baby," Barry pointed out.

The tables outside the village shop were packed with locals taking coffee after the church service. Stopping to exchange greetings with Vangelis and Athena, all done up in their Sunday best, Barry dropped the bombshell that they would officially become godparents next Saturday. Completely unfazed by the news that the baptismal ceremony would take place at such short notice, the couple appeared overjoyed. Embracing Barry and smothering him with kisses, Athena immediately declared *"tha pao stin poli kai tha agorasa ta panta,"* meaning she would go to town and buy everything.

"*Ti ta panta?*" Barry queried what 'everything' was. He was clearly perplexed when Athena continued, "*Ta lathopana, o stavros vaptimatos, oi martyries…*"

"Barry, you not to know the custom for the *Ellinko* baptism, you must to have the oil sheet and the towel, the baptismal cross and the witness pins," Vangelis explained. "Athena will to arrange all; it is the custom for the *nona* to do it. Now you must sit and take the coffee and cake…"

"We really can't, we need to head back and tell Cynthia about the baptism," I protested, my stomach recoiling in horror at the giant portions of honeyed *baklava* on their table and imagining Athena attempting to force feed me the sickly cake. I really wasn't sure if my belt could be loosened any further.

Reaching Barry's house we followed the sound of raised voices out to the ecological pond where we discovered Anne and Lester Trout reclining on a couple of sun loungers and going at each other hammer and tongs. It really was an idyllic setting now that the swimming pool was gone, white water lilies floating on the surface of the ecological pond and the bloom of blue pickerals nosing through the water. Unfortunately the soothing sounds of chirping pond life were rather drowned out by the Trout's continuing argument, the vile couple seemingly oblivious to our presence.

As we arrived on the scene Anne was stridently voicing her opinion that if they just hung around a little longer she might be able to guilt Cynthia into returning to England with them.

"As our only child Cynthia must be made to realise she has a duty to move back to England. Once she's back home with us she'll surely realise what a mistake it was to set up house out here in the middle of nowhere with that common labourer..."

To my surprise Lester appeared to defend his daughter, saying "Well she's done a bit more than just set up house with him, she married him and had his baby..."

"But there's less stigma surrounding divorce these days," Anne said

"That's true, and if Miles takes her on she won't have to bear the shame of being a single mother," Lester added.

"Once we introduce her to Miles I'm sure she will be persuaded to see the error of her ways and realise that he will be a much more suitable husband...you know how keen Jeremy and Cecilia are to see Miles respectably married and it will definitely help you secure that seat on the board," Anne continued.

"But there's no saying that Cynthia will take to Miles," Lester argued. "You know what an odd looking bod he is, that's why he never married."

"Which is why Jeremy and Cecilia are so desperate to find him a wife. I shall remind Cynthia that looks are just superficial, it's breeding that counts. I'm sure Cynthia won't be so selfish as to stand in the way of your promotion to the board, but we only need to mention that as a last resort if she doesn't see reason," Anne wheedled.

"You're right, it would be extremely selfish of her to stand in my way, I do deserve a seat on the board," Lester agreed.

"There's certainly no shame in using our connections to advance your career, all the best quality people do it...oh Barry, I didn't see you there," Anne Trout cried out. Her face flushed with guilt she was clearly trying to work out how much of her poison we had overheard.

"Evidently," Barry snapped, glaring daggers. "Where is Cynthia?"

V.D. BUCKET

"She went over to Marigold's house to collect the baby," Anne replied meekly.

"Anne was just saying that we must treat you and Cynthia to a traditional home cooked English Sunday lunch," Lester said, the lie tripping off his tongue like treacle as his twitch went into overdrive.

"Yes indeed, I was just saying we must pop over to that little shop for a joint of beef," Anne said, a worried expression on her face as she glanced over at Barry. My brother-in-law gazed off into the distance, his silence clearly unnerving his in-laws. Amazingly Barry maintained his composure, a remarkable feat considering the contemptible scheming he had just overheard. Only the almost imperceptible throbbing at one side of his temple indicated to me that he was close to boiling over, but rather than revealing his anger in a fit of temper he chose to reduce his in-laws to size with some choice scathing words.

"Perhaps you can pick up a more suitable husband for Cynthia at the shop," Barry said, his voice dripping with contempt. "You might get lucky with a two for one offer on quality husbands; after all I expect that you picked up this pathetic twitching specimen of manhood on special offer somewhere."

Unable to hold my tongue a moment longer I added "But Barry you forget that Lester is banned from the shop for stealing."

"You promised you'd keep your mouth shut about that," Lester erupted, turning puce as he jumped up from his sun lounger.

"It's a bit late for that, it's all round the village already," I scoffed.

"Not again, you stupid little man. Can't you keep your rampant kleptomania under control for five minutes?" Anne screeched at her husband. "For goodness sake it will be prison you'll be facing rather than a seat in the boardroom if this gets out."

I was shocked to discover that Lester's pilfering was a common habit that his wife was all too familiar with. However her next tirade indicated it was a habit she had no intention of allowing to become public.

"That's it, we're leaving at once, I can't possibly stay here if everyone knows what you've been up to, I'll never live it down if the foreign police cart you off. Lester, come and sort out the suitcases this minute," Anne screamed, storming off.

Unable to look Barry in the eye Lester stared

at the ground shamefaced, meekly asking "Does Cynthia know?"

"I hope not for her sake," Barry replied. "It may be common knowledge in the village but the locals are very fond of Cynthia and will no doubt try to spare her feelings by keeping it from her."

"I'd best go and pack then. Can you call me a taxi to take us to the bus station?"

"Don't you think you owe your daughter some kind of explanation before you slink off?" Barry asked.

"We'll tell her there's an emergency we have to get back to..." Lester muttered before following his wife to sort out their suitcases.

"Do me a favour Victor," Barry said. "Can you pop back to yours and ask Cynthia to come home with the baby. She'd never get her head round it if her parents take off without saying goodbye. I'd go myself but I want to make sure none of our belongings end up in their suitcases."

"Of course," I agreed. "And Barry don't take anything they said to heart, they are nothing but despicable shallow social climbers. Cynthia won the lottery when she met you."

"I'll just be glad to see the back of them. What

a pity you and Marigold can't be surrogate grandparents instead of that foul pair."

"Oh I think you know we'll gladly step into the roles in all but name."

Chapter 22

Painful Peeling

On my return home, I found Marigold and Cynthia relaxing in the garden, the baby sleeping peacefully in the shade of the leafy fig tree. Not wishing to alarm Cynthia by blundering in with the announcement that her parents were packing for an immediate departure, I rather fudged the issue by telling them that Papas Andreas had agreed to baptise Anastasia on Saturday. Naturally both women flew into a panic at the thought of making all the arrangements on such short notice.

"Athena, in her role of godmother, is going to organise all the things you need," I volunteered.

"But Anastasia has nothing to wear," Marigold cried, ignoring the fact that the baby possessed enough outfits to kit out a shop.

Realising that for some inexplicable reason I was still holding the gift which Kyria Maria had made for the baby, I passed the tissue wrapped package to Cynthia.

"Another knitted monstrosity..." Cynthia began to say before exclaiming in delight as she discarded the wrapping. "Oh my, this is just exquisite."

Instead of the expected woolly offering Maria had crafted a beautiful fancy dress with a matching headband.

"Oh look at the whimsical ruffles...and the embroidery, such needlework, it is a work of art," Marigold exclaimed.

"I think the skirt is gossamer organza, and look the waist sash and headband are silk," Cynthia gushed.

"It must have taken Maria hours to stitch these delicate rose appliques," Marigold said. "Well it looks as though Anastasia has something to wear for her christening after all."

Still unsure how to broach the subject of the Trouts imminent departure without provoking one of Cynthia's hysterical bouts of weeping, I was relieved when she popped indoors to change the baby. Alone with my wife I took the opportunity to apprise her of the latest developments.

"The nerve of that woman calling Barry a common labourer when she is nothing but a jumped up nobody married to a petty thief," Marigold said, shaking her head in disbelief. "It is quite incredible to think they were hoping to persuade Cynthia to divorce Barry and marry her off to someone they deemed more suitable."

"Quality, don't you know, completely barmy. I know that arranged marriages were prevalent in Greece not so long ago but I never suspected that kind of thing went on in Cheshire," I laughed. "Anyway the upshot is that they're packing now and a taxi is due...I rather think it would be best if you were the one to break the news to Cynthia that the Trouts have to rush back to England immediately."

"I suppose I could break the news more gently than you...you're certainly not always the most tactful Victor," Marigold said.

Still smarting from the bizarre accusation

that I am not renowned for my tact I left Marigold to deal with Cynthia. Dashing upstairs to my office I took the opportunity to do a quick internet search on the prevalence of salmonella amongst the resident Greek tortoise population. Unfortunately no specific figures were available, but my research did confirm my fears that tortoises are well known carriers of salmonella bacteria. Worried that Kyria Maria may contract something nasty from her new pet I decided I would mitigate the risk by popping over the garden wall at regular intervals to give the tortoise a good dousing with dilute disinfectant. At least with the tortoise no longer littering the chicken run with its droppings I had eliminated the risk of Guzim selling salmonella laden manure down on the coast and of the ex-pat contingent coming down with a mass outbreak of food poisoning.

As we drove to the coast Marigold insisted on dissecting everything that had happened by the ecological pond, rather miffed that she hadn't been there to witness events. She chuntered on about how Cynthia would be feeling torn; knowing that Cynthia had endured enough of her parents imposing without lifting a finger to help, Marigold decided Cynthia would now be wracked with guilt over their abrupt departure.

"Better that she feels the odd twinge of guilt rather than learn the truth that they think she has made a disastrous life choice in marrying Barry and that they planned to interfere, and certainly better than finding out that her father is a common thief," I advised. Because I was still struggling to come to terms with the humiliating reality that I had been fathered by a convicted fraudster, I felt the latter point quite keenly. It was only natural that I wished to spare Cynthia from experiencing similar shame.

By the time we finally pulled in at the secluded cove sited at the base of Viros Gorge there was barely any room left to park the car. It appeared the romantic spot was a popular one with people from town piling into their cars for a Sunday outing. Laden down with beach bags I tripped down a steep path to the pebble beach, the sea gently washing onto the natural stones. Steep cliffs abutting the beach featured natural caves and the lapping waves had eroded arches into the huge rocks rising majestically from the sea.

"What an idyllic spot," Marigold gasped. "Just look at the deep turquoise colour of the sea, it's so inviting."

"I'm glad you like it here," I said, wiping the sweat from my brow.

"There doesn't appear to be any sun loungers, I don't fancy sitting on pebbles," Marigold complained, my cue to troop back up the steep track to the car to retrieve the folding deckchairs we kept in the boot. By the time I returned and set the chairs up on the beach my sweat soaked body was ready to join Marigold in the sea and bask in the cooling water.

Floating on my back I admired the view of the gorge in the distance, its almost vertical face carpeted with an abundance of greenery. Despite our walks in the local area we had not yet tackled anything quite so daunting in scale. I recalled reading that there were some interesting trails in the gorge that meandered past Byzantine churches of historical interest and through picturesque villages. I imagined that Felix, as a very keen walker, would be up for the challenge; perhaps he would enjoy my company on his next visit over to scrutinise Sherry's finances.

After a while I adjourned to my deckchair, leaving Marigold to frolic in the water. The combination of macaroni and meatballs on top of the bacon sandwiches weighed heavily on my stomach, making me unnaturally drowsy. The next thing I knew Marigold was shaking me and I was brusquely woken to the excruciatingly painful sting of sunburned skin. I couldn't believe I had fallen asleep in the sun without taking the precaution of adding high factor sunscreen after my swim; it was terribly remiss of me to be so careless.

"Oh Victor, your poor forehead and nose are bright red. You're going to look an absolute sight when they start to peel," Marigold trilled. "Now look who I ran into in the sea, or should I say swam into?"

Looking over Marigold's shoulder I spotted Giannis and Poppy hovering behind her. Giannis all tanned, toned and muscled looked as handsome as a Greek god. Poppy looked picture perfect; in true Greek style her accessories coordinated to match her bikini and sarong. Her milky white skin served as a painful reminder that my own extremities had been slowly roasted like a lamb on the spit whilst I dozed.

"*Prepei na yinete melos yia mesimeriano yevma,*" Giannis called out. It took a moment for my lethargic brain to translate that he was saying we must join them for lunch.

"Yes do. It was so nice of you to invite us to

join you the other evening, now you must join us," Poppy invited, her eyes fixated on my sun reddened nose. "We're off to my parents' house for lunch; Mama and *Yiayia* are wonderful cooks."

"You don't want a couple of old fogeys like us cramping your style," I protested.

"Nonsense, you will feel like a youngster next to my *yiayia*," Poppy assured me. "We'll find you a nice shady spot, it looks as though you've had too much sun already."

"It's quite ironic really," Marigold piped up. "Victor is always giving long-winded lectures on the importance of applying high factor sun screen, yet here he is all red in the face."

Groaning at the prospect of facing yet more food I protested that we couldn't possibly impose, but Marigold overruled me, insisting it would be a lovely opportunity to extend our circle of Greek friends. Wondering if my sun addled brain would cope with comprehending Greek conversation I dutifully packed up our beach things and followed Marigold back up the steep track, laden down like a pack donkey.

As Giannis drew level with me he said "*tha se voithiso*," offering to help. Relieving me of the deckchairs he chucked them over one shoulder as though they were weightless. Marigold cooed admiringly *"eisai toso dynatis."* Pausing in his tracks Giannis frowned at Marigold in confusion, most likely wondering why she had called him a tyrant. *"Simainei oti eisai poly dynatos,"* I clarified, hurriedly clearing up the misunderstanding by explaining she had meant to say he was very strong. Pleased by the compliment Giannis flexed his muscles; filling Marigold in on her latest language faux pas I ignored withering look she fired in my direction.

When we reached the parking area Poppy told me to follow Giannis' motorbike to the next village, advising me to park in the square as the house was at the top of a steep lane and all the available parking would have been snapped up by visiting relatives. My expression must have given away my dismay at the prospect of trooping up another steep track by foot in the scorching sun, but Poppy laughed off my concern, saying we could jump on the back of Giannis' motorcycle.

As I sped along the road attempting to keep up with Giannis' motorbike I told Marigold I really didn't fancy riding pillion on that monstrous machine without a safety helmet. My wife simply laughed off my concern, telling me not to be so stuffy. I suspected she was secretly thrilled at the prospect of wrapping her arms around the muscled Greek god as though she was some kind of overeager tourist groupie.

"Well we can't stay long, don't forget that Cynthia roped me into doing the authentic Greek taverna evening later," I said.

"Stop being such a grouch Victor. It will be fun to spend some time with the youngsters. I didn't complain when you agreed to take off on one of your jaunts this evening."

"I am working tonight," I pointed out.

"Just another excuse for being paid to eat out while you carouse with Barry if you ask me," Marigold scoffed.

"Since when did Barry and I go off carousing?" I chuckled at such a presposterous notion. "Believe me the last thing on my mind is more food, I'm stuffed to the gills."

In my desperate effort to keep up with Giannis' motorcycle I attempted to overtake an Italian plated car moving along at a crawl, worried I was in danger of flouting some traffic law.

"Well if that's all the thanks I get for doing you a slap up breakfast then I won't bother rustling up bacon sandwiches again in a hurry," Marigold said peevishly.

Chapter 23

Flat Out

After parking up in Poppy's village I was forced to stand around wilting in the heat, my sun-scorched skin aflame and itchy, competing with a growing sense of nausea, whilst Giannis whisked Poppy and then Marigold up to the house on the back of his motorcycle. Despite my reservations about the safety aspects of riding pillion without a helmet I felt too drained to tackle the lane on foot. When Giannis returned, I practically fell onto his machine, hoping I wouldn't attract the attention of the local police by flagrantly flouting the helmet law.

Riding pillion proved to be a most unpleasant experience I will certainly be in no hurry to repeat. Clinging onto Giannis for dear life my body was jolted and jarred as the motorcycle sped through a myriad of potholes, throwing up a cloud of red dust. By the time we arrived at our destination a thick layer of said red dust stuck to my sweaty skin and my throat was parched from swallowing the gritty Saharan sand deposited after the last wind storm.

Arriving at a large stone house set in an elevated position commanding magnificent sea views, my legs vibrated unnaturally as I climbed down from the machine, only Giannis' timely intervention preventing me from taking a nasty tumble.

"*Eisai entaxei?*" Giannis asked me if I was okay, a look of worried concern on his face.

"Too much sun..." I began to say before remembering Giannis doesn't understand English and switching to Greek. "*Eicha para poly ilio.*"

"*Ela.*" Giannis kept a firm grip on my arm as he led me into a walled courtyard with a veritable crowd of people squashed in around a huge trestle table. As I shakily sank into a seat between Poppy and Marigold, Giannis called out, "*Autos einai Victor, chreiazetai nero grigora,*" 'this is Victor, he needs water quickly.' Immediately I was swamped with half-a-dozen of Poppy's relatives introducing themselves and pressing glasses of water on me, tutting at the state of my crimson nose and my obvious confusion. An elderly woman who announced she was Poppy's grandmother rushed over, flapping an elaborately decorated folding fan in my face, all the while exclaiming in Greek that the English had no sense at all when it came to the sun. Appreciative of their concern I attempted to quip 'only mad dogs and Englishmen' but in my confused state I scrambled the words, saying "*Mono treloi Ayylika kai helones.*"

"Why are you rambling on about mad English and tortoises?" Marigold hissed.

The rest of Poppy's relatives joined in, censoriously proclaiming it was complete madness the way the English prostrated their bodies on the beaches in the heat of the day instead of sensibly avoiding the sun by staying indoors until late afternoon. The fact that they were all gathered around a sumptuous outdoor feast during the hottest part of the day appeared to have escaped their notice. A general consensus was reached that since I was looking a tad queasy I should be seated in the shade with the other elderly guests. Unable to summon the necessary Greek vocabulary to protest that I was not technically elderly, merely early-retired, I was summarily shifted to the shady end of the table where I found myself sitting next to Poppy's delightful grandmother.

After downing another glass of water a little of my light-headedness began to dissipate. I took stock of my surroundings. The table was positively groaning under the weight of tempting Greek dishes, but the excess of food only served to exacerbate my biliousness. There were about a dozen of Poppy's relatives crammed round the table, though it appeared there was enough food to feed the proverbial five thousand. The introductions had gone over my head, leaving me pretty clueless who anyone was beyond Poppy's grandmother Calliope, who Poppy was named for.

Across the table Marigold was clearly enjoying herself, completely oblivious to my discomfort as she chatted animatedly with Poppy and threw her head back in tinkling laughter as Giannis presumably said something witty. Plonking a plate down in front of me Calliope began to fill it with a mixture of the nearest dishes, fussily instructing me to eat, assuring me I would feel better with some food inside me, "*Fae, to fagito tha sas kanei na niosete kalytera.*" The concerned granny wasn't to know that I was likely to explode if any more food hit my overstuffed stomach.

As Calliope chuntered on, encouraging me to eat, I stared in horror as my plate was filled with olives, feta, and t*omatokeftedes*, fried tomato fritters which Calliope told me were her signature dish. The pile of food began to grow as my plate was heaped with *briam*, the traditional dish of roasted Mediterranean vegetables bursting with potatoes, tomatoes, aubergines, courgettes and onions. A woman whose name I didn't catch leaned over to add a large dollop of *fasolakia* to my plate and my stomach recoiled at the smell of the garlic laden green beans. Passing a dish down to her grandmother, Poppy called over, "Victor, you must taste Mama's *keftedes*, they are absolutely delectable." My stomach lurched as Calliope spooned a generous portion of the meatballs onto my plate.

Not wishing to appear rude in the face of such hospitality I poked at the food with my fork, hoping that a random cat would happen along to which I could discreetly slip the unwanted food. Snippets of Greek conversation washed over me, Poppy and the menfolk talking excitedly about Greece's chances in the upcoming EUFA semi-final between the national team and the Czech Republic. Having no interest in football I zoned out, concentrating on pushing my uneaten mountain of food beneath a scrumpled paper napkin. Not even a sip of wine passed my lips yet I grew increasingly woozy, finally giving in and begging directions to the bathroom.

I will not litter these pages with the unsavoury, nay downright grisly details, of what followed. Suffice it to say that after a while Marigold finally deigned to notice my prolonged absence and came to find me. When there was no response to the rattling of the bathroom door she returned outside to enlist help. Giannis was roped in to break the bathroom door down and I was discovered flat out, and out of it, on the cold tiled floor. Since Poppy's father had medical expertise he was called to assist. As he examined my prostrate form I came around enough to hear him offer a tentative diagnosis, *"nomizo oti echei iliako enkefaliko epesodio,"* meaning I think he has sunstroke.

Between them Giannis and Poppy's father carried me outside, setting me down in the courtyard before lightly spraying my overheated body with a hosepipe. As I slowly began to revive I could hear Poppy assuring Marigold that her father was hosing me to bring my temperature down to ensure my excessive exposure to the sun didn't develop into heatstroke.

"It's lucky that your father is a doctor," Marigold exclaimed.

"Technically he's not actually a doctor, he is a veterinarian." Poppy said, her words compounding my public humiliation.

"Really I feel much better now," I insisted, sitting up and wringing my shirt out. "I'll be as right as rain after a couple of hours sleep."

"It's lucky I never drink during the day since I'll be the one driving us home," Marigold said, dropping in lots of *"signomis"* as she apologised profusely to our hosts.

Poppy's father insisted on driving us down to the Punto, advising me to keep up my fluid intake. As we pulled away I was deeply touched when Calliope pressed her fan into my hands, telling me my need was greater than hers and depositing a kiss on my sunburnt forehead.

Chapter 24

Authentically Greek

"Your mother is on the telephone, Victor," Marigold said, shaking me awake. "Are you feeling any better dear?"

"How long have I been sleeping?" I asked with a yawn, surprised to find myself flat out on the bed at home. Pickles was curled up next to me on Marigold's pillow, the air conditioner blasting cool air. I reflected that the cat was not exactly a good judge of character if it expected me to wrestle with a tin opener and a can of sardines while I was still suffering the after effects of a dodgy stomach.

"You've slept the afternoon clean away, Barry had to carry you up from the car," Marigold filled me in. Yanking a thermometer out from under my armpit she pronounced my temperature was now at a normal setting. "Shall I tell Vi you'll call her back?"

"Yes, let me just jump in the shower first," I said stretching languidly as Marigold rushed back to the phone. Considering how dreadful I'd felt earlier I appeared to have made a most remarkable recovery.

"Drink this water before you move, the veterinarian recommended you keep topped up with plenty of fluids," Marigold urged on her return. "Are you sure you're feeling better? You certainly look much improved?"

"I feel fine apart from my burnt bits," I assured her, cringing at the unhygienic sight of Pickles licking up the skin peelings littering my pillow.

"Your nose is shining like a beacon but I should be able to disguise the worst of it with some dabs of my green face powder, it works wonders on crimson bits. It's so unlike you to be so careless about sun protection."

BUCKET TO GREECE (VOL. 6)

"I should never have forced down Kyria Maria's macaroni and meatballs…"

"You think it was a touch of food poisoning?" Marigold asked. "Goodness only knows where Maria sticks her fingers before she starts cooking."

"No, just an over indulgence of food, so foolish of me but you know how impossible it is to refuse Greek hospitality without causing offence. If I hadn't eaten such a surfeit of food I would never have dropped off in the sun."

"We must stick to beaches with sun umbrellas in future," Marigold said. "It's a pity your funny turn cut our lunch short, Poppy's family were delightful and so hospitable. You were just lucky that Poppy's father had medical knowledge and was up on the best treatment to cool you down quickly."

Reddening at the recollection that I had been tended to by an animal, rather than human doctor, I suggested we call on his services the next time Marigold's pampered felines needed treatment. Checking the time I realised I needed to be getting ready for work; there was barely time to jump in the shower and return Violet Burke's call.

"I think you need to swerve work this evening

Victor," Marigold advised. "You don't want to risk a relapse."

"I gave my word Marigold. Have you ever known me once pull a sickie in my long and illustrious career as a public health inspector? It just isn't professional."

"You're not working for the council now, you're repping. Tonight isn't one of the tours that you put so much preparation into, it's only a tourist night out," Marigold pointed out. "Let me telephone Cynthia and see if she can cover for you…"

"I'll be fine," I insisted.

"There's no need to play the martyr, Victor. I'd rather you didn't go, but if Cynthia can't do it I will tell Barry he must drive."

Staring in the bathroom mirror I was taken aback by my grotesque reflection, my swollen forehead and nose looking even worse than they felt. Reluctant to let Marigold loose on my face with her doubtless bacteria laden green powder I realised I would be a complete laughing stock if I didn't allow it. My wife has the most unfortunate habit of hoarding date-expired old makeup with no regard to the detrimental dermatological consequences of slapping potentially germ infested products on her skin, arguing that one never knows when a particular shade will be back in fashion. Despite her atrocious habit of hoarding such gunk, in her defence she does have lovely skin: I suspect mine may be a tad more sensitive to date-expired bacteria ridden gloop.

The last time the green face powder had an airing was when Geraldine overdid the sun almost two years ago. I shuddered at the prospect of it coming into contact with my skin, aware that any mould spores would lurk unseen, cleverly disguising themselves by blending into the product colour wise. Still there seemed to be no other option; it was either risking an acne like rash with an application of Marigold's gunky old powder or appearing in public doing a passable imitation of a lobster. That would do my reputation as a seasoned Greek resident no good.

"You really should try vinegar on that sunburn," Barry said for the umpteenth time, dispelling the illusion that Marigold's green powder had worked the wonders she'd promised. The two of us were seated in the taverna that the tour company advertised as promising 'an authentic Greek evening in a traditional setting' waiting for the minibus of eager tourists to arrive.

From our table we could hear the repetitive ping of a microwave oven bleeping, reinforcing the impression I had already formed from the laminated menus with their garish photo images of food that the kitchen may not be as traditional as it was hyped. Looking around I noticed that the tables lacked the traditional condiments of oil and vinegar: I doubted their absence had anything to do with hygiene precautions since oil and vinegar were touted, in pictorial form on the menu, as optional extras at vastly inflated prices. I had already warned Barry to avoid any wine, having caught the taverna owner diluting the bottled contents on my way to the bathroom.

Although I had heard good things about the food here I began to suspect that I'd heard nothing more than clever marketing rumours. When I actually thought about it I realised that Tiffany had been responsible for selecting the taverna as an ideal venue for the authentic excursion, the same Tiffany who would be incapable of spotting the difference between a *saganaki* and a *saliggaria*, even if a snail managed to slither out of the latter and leave a slime trail on the fried cheese.

Sakis had just telephoned my mobile to say he would be a tad late arriving. He explained he'd had problems ticking everyone off the list because the evening's revellers was a party of Germans and Sakis didn't speak a word of the lingo. He was currently parked up outside a petrol station waiting for one of the German men to emerge from the restroom; he was getting worried because the tourist had been gone for a good twenty minutes. I had advised Sakis to at least rattle the door to ensure the bathroom blocker wasn't sprawled on the floor.

Recalling my own earlier unpleasant experience I felt grateful that I had been struck down in a hygienically clean bathroom that was clearly well bleached, rather than in a petrol station lavatory with a filthy floor harbouring dubious puddles and a rank bin overflowing with used toilet paper. Of course I may be slanderously projecting the appalling conditions of this taverna bathroom onto the petrol station, which may well maintain pristine conditions. The revolting state of the toilets here had stuck in my mind since I'd had the misfortune to require the facilities on several occasions since our arrival.

"Seeing that Sakis is delayed with the tourists

we have a few minutes to map out some provisional sketches for your downstairs storage," Barry suggested. "That's if you're feeling well enough. I did promise Marigold I wouldn't allow you to over exert yourself."

"I'll be fine if I stick to water and don't touch any food," I assured him. Even if I hadn't been off my food the lurid orange photograph of this establishment's supposedly 'homemade' *taramasolata* would have put me off. I dreaded to think what went on in the kitchen that would turn the traditional pink fish roe dip into a neon Tango. "It's very good of you step up at the last minute Barry and volunteer to take charge of the tourists."

"Volunteered into it more likely, it's not as though I was left with a choice. I can't say I'm looking forward to it, it's a bit out of my comfort zone, but Marigold will have my guts for garters if you go collapsing again. I have to tell you it was no fun lugging you up a flight of stairs, it was a good job Vangelis was there to grab your feet," Barry said. I flushed in embarrassment at the image: Marigold had neglected to fill me in on that little detail. By now the news of my collapse would be all round the village. "Still I suppose there can't be much to this repping malarkey when it comes to a night out, it's not as though they'll expect me to give one of your long winded lectures full of tedious historical facts. I imagine they'll only be interested in knocking back the ouzo and stuffing their faces."

It struck me that Cynthia must have failed to mention to Barry that he would be expected to lead the Greek dancing and be something of an expert in the ancient Greek art of plate smashing.

Returning Violet Burke's telephone call earlier I was surprised by how down in the dumps my mother sounded. Whilst not wishing to burden me with her problems she had finally confided that the developer had been given the go-ahead and her home and workplace was now scheduled for demolition, despite a petition against it.

"There's no fighting against corrupt councillors accepting back-handers, even if it does leave me on the scrap heap. With the chippy shut down I doubt people will be queuing up to employ me at my advanced age," Violet Burke had said pragmatically. "Tell me what's going on in Meli son; I could do with some cheering up."

I filled my mother in on all the local news and confided my fears about meeting my half-brother Douglas the next day. "Let's hope he doesn't take after your feckless father. He looked normal enough at the funeral, not like that idle chancer who was the double of you."

Since my mother still sounded out of sorts I attempted to lift her spirits by telling her about Anastasia's imminent baptism.

"Ooh I wish I could be there, I expect the Greeks put a bit more of a show on than the Methodists. I'd like to see it and you know how I love a good excuse to wear a nice hat," my mother said wistfully.

Without giving it a second's thought I responded "Why don't you come over for a visit, it could be just the tonic you need? I'll treat you to a plane ticket. Maria was only asking about you this morning and *Kapetanios* Vasos has extended an open invitation for you to enjoy free trips out on Pegasus."

"The mucky old bugger just fancies having his cabin scrubbed…" Vi chuckled.

"Really Mother, a break would do you the world of good and take your mind off your worries. I tell you what; I'll even spring for a new hat for you to wear next Saturday."

BUCKET TO GREECE (VOL. 6)

"I have to say I'm sorely tempted…"

"Leave it with me Mother, I'm going to hang up now and look for a ticket online. I'll call you back as soon as I've sorted something." I have to admit I was astonished that for once she didn't put up her usual argument that she wasn't a charity case, too proud to accept hand-outs.

Although there were no flights into our local airport until the following Sunday I managed to snap up a ticket for Vi to fly from Manchester to Athens on Thursday. My mother didn't sound too impressed when I called her back with the news, complaining that the bone-rattling bus journey from Athens would likely finish her off. "There won't be any leg room to stick my swollen feet up; you know how they blow up on the plane."

"Leave it with me Mother, I may have a way you can avoid the bus trip," I said, suppressing a snort as the gruesome image of my mother's feet exploding mid-flight came to mind, with random toes landing in the in-flight meals of her fellow passengers.

I had something in mind which was easily sorted with another quick call, before phoning Violet Burke back with the details. With everything sorted satisfactorily I finally broke the news to my wife. To her credit Marigold didn't bat an eyelid when I informed her that Violet Burke would be taking over our spare room again; I do believe she is growing quite fond of my mother. However when Marigold heard the arrangements I had made to get my mother from Athens to Meli she sent me a withering look and accused me of being a witless fool.

"Really Victor, do you never think? Spiros has been so looking forward to a romantic reunion with Sampaguita and now you've gone and ruined it."

"How so? Spiros assured me that he didn't mind collecting my mother from the airport, after all he's going to be there anyway to meet Sampaguita. He may as well kill two birds with one stone."

"Well Spiros is unfailingly obliging, as well you know, but you shouldn't have taken advantage. Surely it must have dawned on you that squashing Violet Burke in between Spiros and Sampaguita in the hearse could be the kiss of death for any chance of them rekindling their romance," Marigold chided.

"On the contrary, mother may be the perfect

ice-breaker if things are still a tad strained between them," I protested, belatedly realising that I had indeed been a tad tactless in persuading Spiros to collect Violet Burke.

"Must you be so dense Victor? Violet Burke is most definitely a passion killer."

"Perchance Spiros will have already proposed before mother's flight lands," I said hopefully, though even to my ears my feeble reasoning sounded pathetically lame. Perhaps I could have a quiet word with Spiros and persuade him the romantic thing to do would be to sweep Sampaguita off her feet by getting down on one knee and whipping the gaudy diamond engagement ring out in the airport terminal, before Violet Burke could put the kibosh on any passionate reunion. I doubted that Spiros would spend any time worrying that the terminal floor had been recently mopped; he wasn't so precious about his appearance or random germs. I reflected that since I have a better track record than Spiros in successful relationships he would surely value my advice.

"So I was thinking about the room layout for the storage area. Your mother won't take up too much room. We could divide the floor space so that you retain some storage," Barry's words brought me back to the present and I took a look at his sketch. "Have you mentioned it to Marigold yet?"

"I thought I'd sound my mother out first, no point getting Marigold all riled up if nothing is going to come of it," I said, rather wishfully hoping Marigold would take pity on my mother and be the one to suggest moving her into our downstairs storage. If I feigned reluctance Marigold would be sure to dig her heels in and go out of her way to persuade me it was an excellent idea. "Is it a massive job?"

"The structure's sound, the biggest job will be any rejigging of the water pipes and electrics. We could make it nice, it's lovely and cool down there. I was thinking a cosy living room overlooking the street so your mother can keep her eye on village comings and goings, with a compact kitchen at one end for her chip pan, and a bedroom in the back. It could even bring in some handy income if you rent it out as a holiday let when your mother is back in England."

"I can't imagine Marigold being too thrilled at the prospect of cleaning up after tourists."

"You could get Guzim on the job," Barry suggested.

"Guzim is hardly renowned for his exacting hygiene standards…"

"Not for his personal hygiene admittedly, but you have to give credit where it's due, he keeps those chickens of yours lovely and clean."

"That's all well and good if any passing tourists fancy spending the night in the chicken coop, but Guzim has an even more lackadaisical approach to mopping than Dina, and that's saying something," I said, a mental image of the scummy tidemark the Albanian shed dweller had left in my outdoor bath flashing through my mind.

"I really think you ought to let Marigold in on your plans about the storage, it's never good to keep secrets from your other half," Barry advised.

"That's a bit rich considering you are keeping Lester's shop lifting antics a secret from Cynthia," I reminded him.

"It's a good job I am. Cynthia was still hysterical when I left this evening, without hearing that little bombshell. That parting lecture her poisonous mother gave about how she was chucking away her chance for a decent life by moving to the back of beyond with the likes of me, really upset Cyn. For the life of me I can't understand why she lets herself get so worked up over the disapproval of that obnoxious pair...it's a good job Marigold went over to console her, I'm glad that she's not alone this evening."

"Hmm." Cynthia's incessant waterworks had left her in no fit state to stand in for me this evening. Although Marigold hadn't been looking forward to mopping up Cynthia's histrionics she had gone over to offer a shoulder to cry on, never able to resist a chance to cuddle the baby.

"Are you sure you don't want to put some vinegar on your hooter? Once it gets dark it's going to glow like a beacon," Barry said.

"Hopefully no one will notice if I keep my back turned," I snapped, my patience wearing thin at the constant references to my peeling nose.

Our conversation was interrupted by Makis, the bearded middle-aged taverna owner, marching over to enquire about the delay. Barry and I struggled to keep our faces straight at the sight of the scowling Makis all togged out in a ridiculous knee-length toga. The costume looked as though it had been hacked out of an old curtain; sweeping over one shoulder it revealed far too much of Makis' hairy chest and his decidedly knobbly knees. He posed a real sanitation risk if his chest hairs fell into the food he was serving.

I shuddered as I recalled that Cynthia had expected me to expose myself to similar ridicule by donning an identical costume for the evening, something she had very conveniently neglected to mention until the very last moment when Barry and I were about to leave. I put my foot down and flatly refused to part ways with my dignity for the pittance the job paid. Cynthia's pleas left me unmoved. Nothing could induce me to pose as a shabbily dressed ancient Greek; it was too tacky for words, even more humiliating than the orange indignity of the previous year. I chortled inwardly at my rather witty mental comparison of being Togo'd rather than Tango'd.

Marigold had my back: she took one look at the terrible toga and announced she would divorce me if I dared to make a display of myself in public in such a frightful garment. Her support made me realise it was a good job I hadn't managed to squash myself into one of her dresses for the ritual celebration at the end of the grape harvest; she would never have let me forget such a humiliation.

"The mini-bus should be here anytime now," I told Makis. Considering that he touted the evening's entertainment as authentically Greek he ought to embrace a little tardiness since it was in perfect accord with Greek time-keeping.

"It is really not the good, the tour office tell me the eight o'clock, with this late the chef he complain the oven chips are the dried up," Makis shouted.

"Oven chips, frozen I bet," Barry scoffed as Makis flounced off. "That hardly sounds authentic."

"I think Makis' claims to authenticity are decidedly spurious," I said, rather suspecting the chef was an illegal Albanian that Makis had picked up from the bus stop.

"I suppose I'd better slink off to the toilets and slip into this little number before the crowds arrive," Barry winced, holding aloft the toga I had refused to wear. "If you weren't feeling so off I'd never have agreed to this. It's just a good job I've got the body to carry it off."

Chapter 25

Salvaged from the Bins

"What on earth is keeping Marigold?" I muttered to the chickens as I topped up their water bowls from the watering can. I was anxious enough as it was about my imminent meeting with my half-brother Douglas and his family, without making a bad impression by being tardy. I regretted paying so little attention to Douglas at Vic's funeral that I was left with only a vague impression of my newly discovered sibling, leaving me wondering what to expect when we met up.

V.D. BUCKET

I recalled Douglas had seemed pleasant enough, but my memories of the day were rather dominated by my disreputable half-sibling Terrance and his over-bearing bulbous mother Barb Foot. Confiding in Marigold that the best I could hope for was that Douglas turned out to be less ghastly than the rest of the unsavoury shower who'd turned out for the funeral, my wife had dismissed my worries, saying that Douglas and his family couldn't possibly trounce the Trouts in the awfulness stakes.

"This is your chance to fill in a few of the gaps in your family history," Marigold said, assuring me she was more than curious to meet the extended members of the Bucket family who had flown into Greece the previous day.

My musings were disturbed by Guzim hurrying over, an exceedingly smug expression plastered on his face as he asked *"Thelis na deite ti vrika stous kadous skoupidion?"*

In truth I had not the slightest interest in seeing what Guzim had dug out of the public rubbish bins, but realising it would be churlish to dismiss him out of hand I feigned an interest: he was clearly thrilled with his find. As Guzim brandished his salvaged prize with a flourish I let out an involuntary snort at the sight of the toga Barry had chucked in the bins at the end of the previous evening. Ignoring my incredulous expression Guzim proclaimed *"tha moiazo me enan archaio Ellina se afto."*

"In your dreams," I chuckled, thinking it would take more than Barry's discarded costume to make Guzim look like an ancient Greek.

"Ti?" What, Guzim questioned, clueless I had made a disparaging remark.

"Tha einai chrisimo yia ena fantachtero forema." I attempted to keep a straight face as I told him it would be useful for a fancy dress party.

My mind boggled when Guzim retorted that he planned to wear it for Luljeta to impress her with his manliness. A toothless grin and a wink that reminded me of Lester's twitch accompanied Guzim's hope that his wife would think he looked sexy in the toga. The shabby costume had certainly done nothing for Barry, even though my brother-in-law is becoming quite muscular from all the manual work. I could only imagine how ridiculous the puny Guzim would look in it. I winced at the thought of the Albanian couple donning kinky costumes, but perhaps that accounted for Guzim's ever increasing family. If memory served me correctly Luljeta was currently pregnant with their fifth. Despite their desperate poverty they continued to breed like the rabbits they farmed in their homeland.

Letting himself into the chicken coop and grabbing a rake Guzim glumly informed me the tortoise was still missing *"i helona leipei akoma."* Before I had chance to respond he was off on a guttural rant, accusing the horrible old woman next door of stealing it. Embarrassed that my actions had resulted in such slanderous slurs against my neighbour I rushed to defend her good name; after all I knew for a fact she was innocent. I once again insisted the tortoise in Maria's garden was not the same one as Frappé. Throwing the rake to the ground in a fit of petulance, Guzim folded his arms together and opened his mouth to protest. Nothing came out: instead of spewing accusatory words Guzim simply gawped at my head, finally asking what happened to me. His perpetual habit of staring at the ground as he spoke had spared me an inquisition until now.

"Para poly ilio." Too much sun I explained.

"Ochi to kokkino, to megalo kopsimo?" Guzim replied, saying 'not the red, the big cut?' Before I had chance to answer his question he started rambling on, speaking so quickly I had trouble

translating. Without pausing for breath he speculated on a choice of grisly scenarios that may have befallen me to result in such an unsightly injury, imagining my head had come into close contact with the rooster's spurs, that I had been set upon by unscrupulous brutal muggers who he sincerely hoped weren't compatriots of his, or that I had slipped and cracked my head open trying to get out of the outdoor bath.

Since I considered it none of Guzim's business that I had been walloped in the head by a random shard of flying plate chucked by an over enthusiastic German tourist during the previous evening's authentic Greek experience, I simply retorted *"tha prepei na deis ton allo antra."* Upon hearing me declare 'you should see the other fellow' Guzim's mouth gaped open to such an extent that not only did it expose his toothless gums but I swear I could see his tonsils. He clearly found the notion that I had been involved in a fight, and come off better than the other chap, too preposterous to comprehend: certainly the idea was out of character since I would never engage in public brawling.

The previous evening's tourist excursion was one I had no intention of ever repeating, no matter how much Cynthia cajoled or turned on the waterworks. It certainly ranked as the most inauthentic Greek experience I had ever suffered: the only authentically Greek thing in the place had been the ceramic plates that were broken, Makis defying the edict that for health and safety purposes only replica plaster plates should be smashed. Since I had still been feeling a tad off-colour I had not sampled the food, but Barry was less than impressed with the frozen oven chips served with inadequately defrosted frozen meatballs.

Despite my utter disdain for the whole phoney event the party of German tourists had been in their element, eager to knock back the ouzo, smash plates, and throw themselves into Greek dancing. By the time the dance music started Makis was nowhere to be found so Barry was forced to lead the Greek dancing. Being clueless to any of the footwork needed to successfully dance the *sirtaki*, Barry managed to convince the impressionable group that the conga was a traditional Greek dance as he strutted his stuff at the front of the line. I could only assume that the conga wasn't a popular dance in Deutschland or that the Germans had knocked back too much ouzo to notice there was nothing remotely Greek about it. Even though my brother-in-law had thrown himself into the event with fake enthusiasm, making a complete prat of himself in the ridiculous toga, the customer satisfaction surveys still came back with negative comments. Makis' frozen chips hadn't fooled anyone.

"Do get a move on Victor or we'll be late." Marigold's words brought me back to the present. Indicating to Guzim that I needed to go, I left him still gawping incredulously at the absurd idea I had been in a fight.

Chapter 26

Finding Common Ground

"Let me just slap a little more green powder onto your nose Victor," Marigold said as I parked the Punto close to the hotel where Douglas and his family were staying. "There, that's the best I can do now while it's still raw and peeling."

"I suppose it won't be too obvious because this nasty gash from the flying plate shard will serve as a distraction."

"It's a pity the iodine I applied gives you a rather grotesque yellow hue…"

"At least its antimicrobial properties will prevent a nasty infection setting in," I said. "Let's just hope the new family don't leap to the misguided conclusion that I've been engaged in a spot of brawling."

"If I was you dear I'd just stick with the fib that you got a bit too close to the rooster's spurs," Marigold advised.

"I suppose Guzim's vivid imagination has its uses after all," I laughed, attempting to disguise how nervous I felt.

"Come on, you can do this. If they turn out to be dreadful people we can make an excuse and leave," Marigold assured me, worriedly adding, "You didn't give them our address, did you?"

There were a few people milling around in the hotel reception where I had arranged to meet Douglas, their smart holiday attire indicating they were ready to enjoy an evening out in the resort's tavernas.

"I can definitely see the family resemblance," Marigold announced, immediately zoning in on a man perched on a stool in the corner: her instinct was correct, it was indeed Douglas. Although it was clear that my brother adopted a similar style of dress to me, seemingly emulating my habit of wearing a tie and socks with sandals, I couldn't for the life of me see what possible physical resemblance Marigold was referring to. It was merely coincidental rather than a familial trait that Douglas' skin happened to be pink and peeling, indicating he had overdone the sun on his first day in Greece.

At our approach my sibling sprang to his feet, shaking my hand vigorously between his own rather damp ones and introducing himself to my wife as Duggie. I instantly recalled my first meeting with him in the back of the funeral car. My first impression was that he was short and jovial, and he certainly appeared most amiable now.

"I hope you don't think I'm overstepping the mark with this being your stomping ground and all that, but I took the liberty of booking us a table for dinner...Elaine and the girls are waiting in the restaurant now, they can't wait to meet you. I've told them so much about you," Douglas gushed eagerly. Unfortunately Marigold was not in the position to say the same since I had been terribly remiss by not making any effort to get to know Douglas.

To my shame I knew nothing about the family

BUCKET TO GREECE (VOL. 6)

he was holidaying with since I hadn't even bothered to find out the names or ages of what apparently were my nieces. For the first time it struck me that by viewing Douglas simply as a source of information about my deceased father Vic, I was perhaps missing an opportunity to develop close and fulfilling relationships with my newly discovered family. Of course it was only prudent to be cautious; for all I knew Douglas' family could turn out to be as ghastly and money-grubbing as that uncouth lot in Macclesfield. Then again the relationship could end up as rewarding as the one I had developed with Violet Burke.

Returning from the bathroom I stood to one side, allowing the waiter adequate elbow room to serve the nearest table. Whilst I hovered I looked over to our table, watching Marigold engaged in animated conversation with Elaine. The two women were getting along splendidly, Marigold in an excellent mood because Douglas had selected her favourite restaurant, the one that actually used fancy cloth tablecloths rather than throwaway paper ones. My two six-year old twin nieces, Tilly and Millie, were not only an utter delight but a credit to their parents, demonstrating remarkable table manners for children so young.

Douglas and I had chatted over the *meze* appetizers, slowly getting to know one another. I had correctly pegged Douglas as a rather reluctant paper shuffling office bod, but was rather taken aback to learn he had chucked it in to become a house-husband while Elaine brought home the bacon. Of course it transpired that bacon was the last thing Elaine actually had anything to do with: in a last desperate attempt to get pregnant before her clock stopped ticking Elaine had devised her own innovative diet plan, shedding a remarkable ten stone. With the birth of the twins she had marketed her diet to great acclaim, becoming quite the successful weight-loss entrepreneur.

By the time the twins were toddling she was raking in so much money that Douglas was able to quit the nine-to-five rat-race and stay at home with the children, whilst helping Elaine with the business by devising tasty new low calorie recipes that added constant variety to the increasingly popular diet meal plan. Douglas was very committed to experimenting with new and exciting flavours to ensure Elaine's ever growing cohort of devoted dieters could burn the belly fat without enduring a constant diet of bland food.

Our mutual interest in cooking meant that Douglas and I had something in common. The revelation that Douglas' recipes would soon feature in a glossy cookery book indicated common literary ground between us, the first draft of my moving abroad saga now at the editing stage. Marigold and Elaine drew attention to something else we had in common, snorting with laughter when Douglas and I both whipped out disinfectant wipes at the exact same moment to expunge any lurking bacteria from the rather dubious looking condiments.

"You can never be too careful," Douglas opined. "It is very rare for restaurants to sanitise the salt and pepper shakers between patrons."

"The oily fingerprint smudges visible on these oil and vinegar bottles indicate a lack of close attention to strict hygienic sterility," I added.

Once the waiter had finished serving I rejoined my family at the table, delighted to see how much Tilly and Millie were enjoying their fresh *kalamari* and *lahanosalata me karoto*. It was so refreshing to see English children tucking into squid, and cabbage salad with carrots, rather than demanding an unimaginative selection of chicken nuggets and fish fingers from the children's menu.

I was gratified that Douglas had insisted that there would be no first name familiarity nonsense; both girls were already politely addressing Marigold and me as Aunty and Uncle Bucket. Over the course of the meal I noticed a tendency for Douglas to defer to me as the elder brother. Although it was a role I had never played before, I supposed I could grow into it. Or course I was also an elder brother to Terrance, but it seemed best to disown him, and to the elusive Jimmy, Vic's fourth son who was the same age as Benjamin. At ten years my junior Douglas was in the middle of the pecking order. It was clear from what he told me that I wasn't the only one to make the sensible decision that Terrance was best avoided.

Whilst the women chatted Douglas filled in a few of the blanks concerning our other half-siblings and our mutual father. It seemed that Vic had established a pattern of seducing women and then shamelessly limping away. Vic exploited his fake injury as part of his seduction technique, having discovered women found it hard to resist his fantasised heroic accounts of how he ended up with a leg full of imaginary shrapnel.

When Vic abandoned Douglas' mum Sharon he left her pregnant and penniless. Heartbroken, Sharon finally tracked the elusive Vic down, only to discover he was actually shacked up with the indomitable Barb Foot. Confronting Barb on the doorstep of the terraced house she shared with Vic, Sharon received short shrift; Barb was certainly an intimidating force to be reckoned with back in the day, even more of a dragon in her younger years than she is now. The bolshie Barb showed not a whit of sympathy for Sharon's predicament. Clad in a garish leopard skin dressing gown, hair rollers poking out of her head scarf and hands staunchly on hips, she epitomised the image of a northern battle-axe. Hurling a foul string of obscenities at Sharon she swore the younger woman would never lure Vic away from her.

The support of a loving family spared Sharon from being forced into the same agonising bucket decision as Violet Burke. Over the years Vic maintained sporadic contact, turning up out of the blue and bunging the odd bit of cash to Sharon, inveigling his way into Douglas' life, the child too young and impressionable to see his father's true colours. When Sharon made a respectable marriage her new husband discouraged any contact with Vic, considering him a disreputable influence on his step-son. Vic made the occasional effort to see his son on the sly, loitering around outside the school at home time with the unfortunate consequence that he was occasionally pegged as a dodgy playground pervert.

"Even though he was an unreliable fly-by night I still cherish one memory of Vic. I was nine and it was the last time I saw him before he was sent down, but of course I was clueless why he suddenly disappeared off the radar," Douglas confided. "It was after school; I'd just bought a thrupenny bag of aniseed balls from the corner shop when Derek Brown swaggered along and threatened to give me a black eye unless I handed them over. I hated Derek Brown, he was a real bully who delighted in making my life a misery. Anyway out of the blue my dad was there, threatening to spread it all around the playground that Derek Brown had been so terrified watching the 'Doctor Who' episode with the poisonous seaweed that he wet himself. The threat of public humiliation was too much for Derek Brown and he never bothered me again. I rather idolised Vic after that, even though it was years before I saw him again."

I was glad to hear that Vic had found an imaginative way to deal with the little thug that had bullied Douglas. Back in my short trouser days I too would have idolised anyone who stepped in and sorted out Derek Little, though it had taken my own ingenuity with a Bunsen burner to neutralise my Little problem. "Of course Elaine didn't want Vic to have anything to do with the twins, knowing he'd set a bad example," Douglas said.

"Well hopefully I can step into the breach and set the girls a good example," I said. "Let's leave the ladies to enjoy their coffee in peace and take the twins down to play on the beach. I have a Derek tale of my own you may like to hear."

The children kicked off their sandals and paddled in the shallows, entranced by the gentle waves washing onto the sand. Douglas and I kicked over old times, reminiscing and catching up on fifty missed years, forming a brotherly bond that boded well for the future.

Chapter 27

A Blissful Soak

"That was such a delightful evening," Marigold trilled as I parked the Punto outside the house, narrowly missing a random stray stretched out in the dark. "I know how worried you've been about meeting up with an unknown half-sibling; after all he could have turned out to be a deranged serial killer, or even worse a jumped-up snob like Lester, but Douglas and his family are just lovely people. I certainly never expected at this stage in our marriage to find a sister-in-law who I can relate to in the same way you do with Barry, and what an unexpected treat to discover we have two such adorable nieces."

"It's certainly a turn up for the books," I agreed, silently regretting not taking the chance to get to know Douglas better at Vic's funeral, but in my defence my mind had been all over the place. I relished the opportunity to make up for lost time during the rest of Douglas' stay.

"I'm so relieved for your sake that the evening turned out so well. In fact I'm so happy that I'm going to do something I never thought I would," Marigold teased, depositing a tender kiss on my cheek. I raised my eyebrows quizzically, wondering quite what Marigold was hinting at. "I'm going to draw you a bubble bath in Harold's monstrous old tub that you parked in the garden."

"You don't want all the bother of fixing a hosepipe to the bathroom sink at this time of night," I bluffed, rather hoping Marigold would insist.

"Darling, you deserve it. A nice long soak will be just the thing to take the sting out of that nasty sunburn."

Bubbles up to my neck I luxuriated in the cast

iron bath tub, reflecting life really didn't get much better than this. The balmy late evening temperature was perfect for my improvised outdoor spa, the moonlight casting its silvery rays across the garden, illuminating the fragrant flowering pot plants and the lighted citronella coils Marigold had thoughtfully placed around the tub to keep the mosquitoes at bay. It was blissfully peaceful, the chickens all shut away in the hen house for the night. Closing my eyes I felt myself drifting at the half-way point between sleep and consciousness, relishing every second of the unique experience. When something plopped in the water I was too relaxed to open my eyes and the bizarre thought that it must be raining crossed my mind.

Another plop disturbed me and I felt something brush against my chest in the water. Opening my eyes I groaned in annoyance; it appeared that my outdoor bath had attracted some of the local frog population that must have migrated over from Cynthia's ecological pond. As the realisation actually hit me that my bath water was infested with frogs I sprang out of the tub, not realising I had an audience.

"*Kolympate kai sto esoroucho sas,*" the guttural voice of Guzim cackled as he accused me of bathing in my underpants too. Grabbing my towel and as much dignity as I could muster, I turned on my heel. Perish the thought that I would bathe in my underpants; the very notion was utterly preposterous. Scurrying across the garden I reflected Guzim really must be dense if he is unable to appreciate the difference between a pair of Y-fronts and the newest line in swimming trunks from Marks and Spencer.

I quickened my pace as a dire thought struck me. Marigold would have kittens if any of the frogs turned up in our bed.

A Note from Victor

All Amazon reviews most welcome.

Please feel free to drop a line if you would like information on the release date of future volumes in the Bucket series at
vdbucket@gmail.com